Witness: One Response to Vatican II

WITNESS:
One Response to Vatican II

Sister Margaret Mary Baney

Foreword by
Cardinal O'Connor

VANTAGE PRESS
New York / Atlanta
Los Angeles / Chicago

FIRST EDITION

All rights reserved, including the right of
reproduction in whole or in part in any form.

Copyright © 1987 by Sisters, Servants of the Immaculate
Heart of Mary

Published by Vantage Press, Inc.
516 West 34th Street, New York, New York 10001

Manufactured in the United States of America
ISBN: 0-533-07210-7

Library of Congress Catalog Card No.: 86-90277

To His Holiness Pope John Paul II,
in Gratitude for
His Inspiring and Courageous Leadership

and

John Cardinal Krol as He Celebrates Fifty Years of Faithful
and Fruitful Service in the Priesthood

Contents

Foreword ix
Introduction xiii
I. Call to Witness: Invitation of Vatican II .. 1
II. Origin of Witness: Charism and Early History 15
III. Extension of Witness: Apostolate 23
IV. Formation for Witness: Professional Preparation 61
V. Exchange of Witness: Community Life and Spirit 77
VI. Sharing of Witness: Collaboration with Other Religious 93
VII. Facets of Witness: Liturgical Prayer 111
Notes 119

Appendices

    A. Superiors General and Councilors .. 133
    B. Bachelor Degrees Earned at Immaculata College by Sisters, Servants of the Immaculate Heart of Mary 135
    C. Master Degrees Earned by Sisters of I.H.M. 136
    D. Colleges and Universities Attended by Sisters, Servants of the Immaculate Heart of Mary 1969–85 137
    E. Teacher Certifcation 143

Foreword

It's a book bursting with pride, that's the best way to describe Sister Margaret Mary Baney's volume, *Witness: One Response to Vatican II*. It's the justifiable pride of the Sisters, Servants of the Immaculate Heart of Mary, and Sister Margaret Mary has captured it very effectively and very beautifully in reviewing some of the experiences of her religious congregation during the past twenty years. With a membership of 1,776 sisters serving in 188 institutions on every level of education and teaching more than 100,000 students in North and South America, it is surely one of the most remarkable success stories of modern religious life, and well deserving of the pride felt by the author and her associates.

But best to acknowledge a prejudice before being accused of it. I am, indeed, prejudiced in behalf of the Sisters, Servants of the Immaculate Heart of Mary, more simply the I.H.M.s. Could I not be, since they staffed my home parish of Saint Clement's in Philadelphia, from before my birth? Could I be unprejudiced toward sisters for whom I celebrated mass each day—if far earlier than I would have lazily liked to—at Saint Thomas More, in Arlington, Virginia? Could I be less than prejudiced in favor of a community that claims two of my beloved Philadelphia blood-cousins, both wonderful religious, wonderful teachers and wonderful cousins? Other associations with the I.H.M.s prejudice me, as well, but I have sufficiently satisfied my scrupulosity, and, I trust, preempted any who might dismiss my comments on Sister Margaret Mary Baney's work were my associations revealed by others without my having issued fair warning. And so to the book.

It is generally agreed that Women Religious in the United States are among the most reflective and "renewed" individuals in the history of the Catholic Church. No group responded with greater alacrity to the repeated summonses of the popes since John XXIII to spiritual renewal and to reflection upon the meaning of commitment to religious life. In the years following the Second Vatican Council, Sisters became as familiar as anyone with such documents as *Lumen Gentium, Gaudium et Spes* and *Perfectae Caritatis*, as well as with several extraordinary communications emanating from the Sacred Congregation for Religious and Secular Institutes. I have no doubt that much of the success of the I.H.M.s, at a time when many were experiencing the serious consequences of internal and external upheaval, came from the fact that their careful study of the documents of Vatican II was accompanied by a special chapter in 1969 which enabled the sisters to crystalize their thoughts and reactions in a volume entitled *Faithful Witness*, which gave direction and stability at a time of change and readjustment. What emerges repeatedly from these pages of historical record is the determined will of the Sisters to be thoroughly updated in the advancing growth and development of the Magisterium reflected in the documents of Vatican II, while retaining their stability, their charism, their tradition. The leadership and the members of this community were welded as one in their loyalty to the Holy Father and in their dedication to all that makes religious life a unique phenomenon in human society.

Impressive, indeed, has been the ability of this community of religious women to persevere in their mission in the years of drastic change which mark these past two decades. New commitments to education were made, and a remarkable facility to combine resources and utilize personnel revealed itself. No identity crisis prevented this group of religious from fulfilling its mission to Christian education, and a strong leadership did not fail to be decisive and responsible for the consequences of the positions that were taken. What is evident, time and again, is the highly professional stance of these Sisters of the Immaculate Heart of Mary. Formation, spiritual as well as academic, is the key to their contribution to the quality of religious life and to the field of education.

Witness in the title of this volume measures more the quality of their contribution than the quantity, and yet if numbers were the sole criterion for success, they would be successful hands down. Fortunately, it is their unswerving dedication to the art of teaching and their unequivocal fidelity to the essential elements of religious life that have preserved their identity during these twenty years since Vatican II. In my judgment, the Sisters of the Immaculate Heart of Mary will be on hand to bear witness to the decrees and exhortations of many future popes and councils. They will be in the forefront of those who, consecrated by baptism and by their vows, "are a splendid sign in the church, as they foretell the heavenly glory" (Can. 573).

I must reflect once more, if but briefly, on my days as a boy growing up in the Archdiocese of Philadelphia and as a priest of that archdiocese for some thirty-three years before being excardinated by way of being appointed a bishop by our Holy Father, Pope John Paul II. Philadelphia has always spelled nostalgia to me, and will, I am sure, until the day I die, despite my love for and loyalty to my adopted Archdiocese of New York. Certain "givens" characterize Philadelphia, in retrospect and in reality, givens of the stuff which generates nostalgia: the loyalty of Philadelphia's priests, the generosity of its people, the dynamic orthodoxy of its religious teachers, its massive Catholic school system, the stability of so many of its religious women. Because of the happenstances of my own life, the pervasive reality of the I.H.M.s—the fact that they were always *there*—makes them stand out in special relief for me, personally, even amidst so many who have contributed so much to the Church in general, and to the church in Philadelphia, in particular. I suspect that even strangers to my home archdiocese will understand my nostalgia, and even experience it vicariously themselves, upon reading this witness of love which describes one response—one glorious response—to Vatican II.

—John Cardinal O'Connor

Introduction

When Pope John Paul II convoked the special Synod of Bishops in Rome in 1985, he specified as one of its objectives: "to promote the further implementation of the Council in the life of the Church." The Bishops in their final statement declared: "We bishops, all of us, together with Peter, and under his guidance, have strived to comprehend more deeply the Second Vatican Council . . . and we commit ourselves to its promotion."

This volume is a review of some of the experiences of one religious congregation during these past twenty years, in the light of the documents of Vatican II. This review includes the areas of prayer, liturgical and private, apostolate, community spirit, and collaboration with other congregations. Other developments remain to be covered in future writings.

My sincere appreciation is due to Mother Marie Genevieve Lawler and the members of the General Council who entrusted this task to me. For their ever gracious cooperation and assistance, I thank the community archivists, Sister Genevieve Mary Simons and Sister Rose Bernard Bernard. I am likewise indebted to the many members of the congregation who supported me in this endeavor, especially to Sister Mary Joseph McAllister who painstakingly prepared the manuscript.

Finally, as Jesus said "Without Me you can do nothing," the composing of this work afforded the opportunity to reflect, with gratitude, on the countless blessings God has bestowed on the activities of the congregation, undertaken for His glory and in honor of the Immaculate Heart of Mary.

Witness: One Response to Vatican II

CHAPTER I

Call to Witness: Invitation of Vatican II

Shortly after Pope John Paul II sent the letter to the bishops of the United States requesting them during the Holy Year to render special pastoral service to the religious of their dioceses, Archbishop John Quinn the Pontifical Delegate, who heads the special commission appointed to facilitate the work, declared: "The purpose of the present action of the Pope is to enable American religious to surface and to reflect on the various ways they have developed since Vatican II. It will enable them to review their experience and structural changes in the light of the teaching of the Church on religious life and in the light of the religious witness they are giving in the American context."[1]

This present work is the story of the development during that period of one congregation, the Sisters, Servants of the Immaculate Heart of Mary, whose motherhouse is located at Immaculata, Pennsylvania. Dedicated to the apostolate of Catholic education, this congregation has a membership of 1,776 including 12 novices and 15 postulants, serving in 188 institutions on every educational level, from Montessori school to graduate programs on the collegiate level. In addition to the schools in Pennsylvania, the sisters also staff institutions in California, Connecticut, Florida, Georgia, Nebraska, New Jersey, North and South Carolina, and Virginia, as well as in Peru and Chile in South America. In the current scholastic year they are teaching more than one hundred thousand students.

In the review of experiences mentioned by Archbishop Quinn, the story should start with Pope John XXIII, who, on July 2, 1962, in his letter to women religious, declared: "This is a solemn hour for the history of the Church. It involves, therefore, increasing the fervor of its efforts for spiritual renewal . . . in order to give new impetus to the works and institutions of its millenial life."[2]

Elucidating still further, he pointed out that "preparation for the council demands that souls consecrated to the Lord according to the forms approved by canonical legislation should reconsider with renewed fervor the commitments of their vocation,"[3] and delineated that vocation as one which is, in reality, a life of prayer, a life of example, and a life of apostolate.

Called upon as were all religious congregations to undertake a complete study of constitutions and life-style, the Sisters, Servants of the Immaculate Heart of Mary began a period of special prayer invoking the light of the Holy Spirit and held a special chapter of affairs with sessions in July 1969, December 1969, and July 1970. In preparation for this chapter, communitywide study focused on the papal pronouncements on religious life, the pertinent documents of Vatican II, particularly *Lumen Gentium, Gaudium et Spes, Perfectae Caritatis, Christus Dominus, Gravissimum Educationis,* the *motu proprio Ecclesiae Sanctae,* and *Renovationis Causam* issued by the Sacred Congregation for

Religious and Secular Institutes by virtue of a special mandate from Pope Paul. With these as guidelines extensive questionnaires were sent to all members, dealing with prayer and spirituality, common life, and apostolate. Precapitular, and in due time capitular, commissions were responsible for drafting the instruments and collating the responses. The entire membership also collaborated in the election of delegates to the chapter.

The adaptation and renewal to which the Council called religious included "both the constant return to the sources of all Christian life and to the original spirit of the institutes, and their adaptation to the changed condition of our time."[4] With this as the goal and with the documents cited above as guidelines, the capitulars enacted changes in the area of prayer and spirituality, consecrated life, apostolate, formation, and government, and consolidated these enactments in a volume titled *Faithful Witness*, which served as interim constitutions during the period of experimentation set up by the Sacred Congregation of Religious and Secular Institutes.

One of the most significant enactments of the 1968 chapter was:

> The Congregation of the Sisters, Servants of the Immaculate Heart of Mary, Immaculata, Pennsylvania, shall remain a Religious Institute as currently defined by the Church, with the norms of:
>
> —Public profession of the vows of poverty, chastity, and obedience.
> —Common life for all members.
> —Distinctive religious habit, visible sign of consecration to God and to the service of God's people.

During the ensuing six years the sisters sought to

deepen their spiritual life and vivify their apostolate, testing the validity of the adaptations and proposing modifications or additions to be discussed at the 1975 chapter.

In this period, the significant document *Evangelica Testificatio*, issued by Pope Paul VI, elucidated further the Council's statements on religious life and served as a standard against which to measure changes. The Pope called all religious to a renewal of the authentic and integral vocation of each institute by maintaining the "stable forms of living" recognized by the Church. He reminded all that: "For a living being, adaptation to its surroundings does not consist in abandoning its true identity, but rather in asserting itself in the vitality that is its own. Deep understanding of present tendencies and of the needs of the modern world should cause your own sources of energy to spring up with renewed vigor and freshness."[5]

Since the spirit of the congregation is rooted in that of Saint Alphonsus, the span of years between these two chapters saw a determined effort to become more truly imbued with it and more knowledgable about Alphonsian writings. Each sister received a personal copy of the life of Saint Alphonsus, *Never Stop Walking*, as well as copies of his works: *The Practice of the Love of Jesus Christ, To Serve Christ Jesus*, and *The Passion of Jesus Christ* (translated from the Italian by Sr. Nancy Fearon, I.H.M. Monroe). Workshops in which the entire community participated were organized first on the subject of Alphonsian spirituality, and subsequently on Sacred Scripture and various aspects of the spiritual life.

In addition to personal study on the part of the sisters, outstanding priests came to Villa Maria Motherhouse to address them and share valuable insights. The members of the community received great inspiration in their efforts to grow in the love of Christ and to spread the good news to others through their contact with such theologians as

Archbishop Luigi Raymundi, the Apostolic Delegate to the United States, Rev. Barnabas Ahern, C.P., Archbishop Fulton Sheen, Cardinal John Krol, Dom Hubert Van Zeller, Rev. Thomas Dubay, S.M., Rev. John Hardon, S.J., Rev. Jude Mead, C.P., Bernard Haring, C.S.S.R., and Archbishop Augustin Mayer, of the Sacred Congregation of Religious and Secular Institutes, to mention only the most widely known.

When Pope Paul VI declared 1975 as a Holy Year, a special spiritual program was designed. It was envisioned as a communitywide project and included the following components:

1—Intensified prayer of all the sisters for a true spiritual renewal in the congregation.
2—A five-week institute in the summer, during which each sister would pursue a course in Sacred Scripture and one in some aspect of spirituality.
3—A visiting lecturer each week of the institute to provide further enrichment in these areas.
4—By special permission, daily exposition of the Blessed Sacrament at Immaculata College during the institute and at Villa Maria by the Sea, the community retreat house.

Immaculata College campus, utilized ordinarily during the summer months for academic courses, was reserved exclusively for the institute on spirituality. Here four hundred sisters, professed thirty-seven to fifty-five years resided for a five-week period and took two courses. In this way the oldest group in the community had exposure to the teaching of Vatican II and new insights into Sacred Scripture. Supplementing the courses on campus were the weekly lectures by eminent scholars.

The remaining members of the congregation lived in

local parishes and were engaged in catechetical instruction and other works of the apostolate. In order that they might participate through independent study, extensive course outlines were provided on two topics: "New Testament Theology: Themes in Saint Paul" and "Contemplative Prayer: Its Source and Power." In addition, they profited by attendance at the weekly lecture series.

Last but not least, three groups of sisters who were engaged in House of Prayer programs that summer concentrated on these same themes in their study projects and in their special prayer.

As the groundwork for the program was being laid, a major concern was to recruit outstanding teachers who would consider the work of the summer not just "giving a course," but as membership in a team working to attain the goals of the institute. Ideally, time spent together beforehand might ensure this, but since the priests were based in areas representing a wide geographic spread, including Europe, this was not possible. However, by the grace of God, this much desired attitude was indeed present, and the priests gave themselves unstintingly to the spiritual development of the sisters through their well-planned courses, their excellent homilies, their willing and valued service as confessors and counselors, and the exemplary spirit of community which developed. Their personal holiness as well as their scholarly competence had a deep influence.

Concurrently, the Chapter of Affairs was in progress, and at the end of the session a new volume of *Faithful Witness* was provided to the community. This differed from the preceding one in that it combined any new elements and enactments of the former chapter with materials retained from the constitutions approved in 1965 at the time of papal approbation. In drafting this work, the capitulars followed the advice of specialists in religious life who advocated that new constitutions combine the spiritual motivation and content with the legal norms. This was in contrast to the format that constitutions had had in the past, since that was judged not to provide the inspiration conducive to growth in union with Christ envisioned by Vatican II. As one authority phrased it: "The jurisprudence of the Holy See had already been calling for brief principles of spiritual and religious life to be placed in the text, especially those that appropriately define the spirit proper to the institute, strengthening and applying it. Now more is asked. The great doctrinal, spiritual, and apostolic guidelines of the Church emphasized by the Council are to be given importance in religious constitutions, too."[6]

The Church in her wisdom wished to allow congregations ample time to test and evaluate proposed changes before finalizing them as a way of life that would achieve the goal of each congregation. Six years remained for experimentation before the chapter of 1981, which would mark for the Sisters, Servants of the Immaculate Heart of Mary the time at which revised constitutions, the fruit of these twelve years of study and application, should be submitted to the Sacred Congregation for Religious for definitive approval.

During these six years, the Catholics of Philadelphia had three tremendous experiences, and the Sisters, Servants of the Immaculate Heart of Mary, shared these historic and grace-filled events. In 1976, the year of the bicentennial celebration of the United States, Philadelphia was privileged to host the Forty-first International Eucharistic Congress. On June 19, 1977, Pope Paul VI canonized the fourth Bishop of Philadelphia, Saint John Nepomucene Neumann. Since he was the Bishop who invited the sisters to Philadelphia in 1858,[7] the community was represented prominently both in the canonization ceremonies in Rome, and in those held at various sites locally. Finally, in 1979, the Catholics of Philadelphia exulted in the visit of Pope John Paul II, the first visit paid to that city by a reigning pontiff. True, Pope Pius XII,[8] then Cardinal Pacelli, had spent a few hours in Philadelphia in 1936, and Pope Paul VI (Cardinal Montini) had toured the city in 1960, visiting Bishop Neumann High School, Rosemont College, and Independence Hall.[9] Pope John Paul II, as Cardinal Wojtyla, had been present in 1976 for the Eucharistic Congress. In the preparation for the beautiful liturgies offered during these occasions the sisters considered it a privilege to participate in various ways, especially as sacristans and choir directors.

Within the congregation, the period preceding the final special chapter of 1981 saw an intensification of prayer and study. By popular demand, the institute on spirituality inaugurated during the Holy Year was repeated each succeeding summer. Each year it became increasingly evident that the program was filling a real need, and that the sisters were profiting immensely from the hours of prayer before their Eucharistic King. In addition to the inspiration and intellectual challenge of the classes, they found great joy in community sharing.

During the ten years of the program, the faculty and guest lecturers have included several members of the diocesan clergy, as well as representatives from the following religious congregations: Franciscan, Jesuit, Stigmatine, Redemptorist, Holy Ghost Fathers, Benedictine, Dominican, Marist, Oblates of St. Francis de Sales, Capuchin, Vincentian, and Passionist. These men hold degrees not only from distinguished universities in the United States but also from those in Paris (Insitut Catholique and University of Paris), Jerusalem (Dominican Biblical and Archaeological School), Louvain, Fribourg, and Rome (Pontifical Lateran,

Angelicum, Teresianum, Biblical Institute, and Gregorian).

As well as being effective teachers, the faculty members were also productive scholars and among the group they have published ninety books and have contributed to the *New Catholic Encyclopedia, The Jerome Biblical Commentary,* and *Encyclopedic Dictionary of Religions.* Their articles have appeared in numerous periodicals, including *America, Catholic Biblical quarterly, Homiletic and Pastoral Review, Journal of Ecumenical Studies, The Catholic Lawyer, Catholic Historical Review,* and *Communio.*

Through this program, as well as through workshops and lectures during the academic year there was an earnest effort to create the atmosphere referred to by Pope John Paul II when he addressed the Superiors General in Rome:

> Your houses must be above all, centers of prayer, meditation and dialogue—personal and of the whole community—with Him who is and must remain the first and principal interlocutor in the industrious succession of your days. If you are able to nourish this "climate" of intense and loving communion with God, it will be possible for you to carry forward, without traumatic tensions or dangerous confusion, that renewal of life and discipline to which the Second Vatican Ecumenical Council committed you.[10]

During these years of preparation, a Vatican document was issued which was of singular importance for all members of the Church, but most particularly for religious whose apostolate is the education of young people—*Catechesi Tradendae.*

Pope John Paul II, commenting on the Fourth General Synod of 1977, which was devoted to the subject of catechesis, stated: "The thought of the Synod Fathers was addressed particularly to the young of whose growing importance in the world of today they were well aware: for amid uncertainties and disorders, excesses and frustrations, the young represent the great force on which the fate of the future of humanity depends."

Noting that the main preoccupation of the Synod Fathers was the effort to discover the means by which young people could be brought to a living experience of Jesus Christ through knowledge of his person and message which becomes more complete each day, he declared that reaching this discovery is the most urgent task of the Church today. Every effort must be made to kindle in our youth "the passion for the kingdom which He came to inaugurate and in which alone the human being can find full and satisfying self-fulfillment."[11]

In this period, the congregation of the Sisters, Servants of I.H.M. examined the apostolate of Catholic education and overwhelmingly reiterated its value in the Church today. Mindful of the words of the Council Fathers, they reaffirmed their work. In reaching this decision they were strengthened by the statements of the bishops of the various dioceses in which they labored, who pointed out in eloquent terms the need for religious in the schools of America. Just as the Sacred Congregation for Education had declared in its documents, *The Catholic School*, that the loss of these schools would be a serious blow,[12] these individual members of the hierarchy spoke for their particular dioceses.

The bishops of the sixteen dioceses in which the sisters labor have been unanimous in voicing their appreciation for the work accomplished in the Catholic schools. As Bishop Thomas Welsh expressed it: "I think that there is no area of Church work where sisters could be of more service than in the education of our young people. With pagan values in public education, with broken homes and with both parents working, the Catholic school is more important than ever. It is our experience that where the I.H.M. Sisters teach we do have Catholic schools."[13]

It is interesting that such a statement was made by the Bishop of Arlington, in view of the public school systems in that area of Northern Virginia which enjoy such a fine reputation and in which the per capita expenditure for education annually is over three thousand dollars, the highest in the state of Virginia. In essence his opinion parallels that of a bishop in the coal-mining areas of Pennsylvania where the students are of a different socio-economic background. The bishop writes:

> The teaching apostolate has been a vital one to the life of our diocese, and your community has played no little part in that special work. The witness that your sisters give as women who live and love their profession of the evangelical counsels is a precious gift our people have enjoyed.... These small towns of the coal regions have been strong centers of Catholic life and faith for many years and so we should do everything possible to bolster their spirit. They have sent many a young man to the altar, and many a young girl to the covent.[14]

So many of the bishops used the words joy, witness and love in describing the work of the sisters in the apostolate of education, and then commented on their professional competence. The Bishop of Harrisburg, Pennsylvania and the Archbishop of Miami, Florida are two cases in point.

> From firsthand knowledge I find your sisters living lives of deep spirituality and displaying a loving, caring regard for one another and the children they direct... It is obvious that you make a concerted effort to supply well-educated and able-bodied teachers.

> Wherever your sisters serve in our diocese they give a lasting impression of a religious educator happy to be serving Almighty God and His Church.[15]

and

> The schools that the Immaculate Heart of Mary Sisters staff in our Archdiocese are among the best anywhere. They give excellent witness to faith and the religious life. The outward witness of the religious habit is a sign of the lived commitment of the Immaculate Heart of Mary Community. As if that were not enough they are teachers *par excellence.*[16]

Another one who struck the note of joy was Archbishop Whealon of Hartford, when he commented: "In my judgment this Community has come through the upsetting conditions of Vatican II in strong fashion. You have kept the basics for a strong Community: a sense of your own community; a superior with authority; the religious habit. Along with that is a willingness to serve the Church, and a spirit of joy in giving that service."[17]

From the Midwest comes the comment: "My main comment is that the I.H.M. Sisters in Saint Joseph School are an inspiration to our priests, laity, and other religious in the city in their living of the vows, and they are showing the people of Saint Joseph parish what is the very best in Catholic education. . . . I pray that you will not change your apostolate. Catholic schools are as necessary today as ever before in our country. The United States needs its women religious in its schools. It always will."[18]

The bishops of the far West echo this same appreciation of the apostolate:

> It has been a great comfort to me, as well as to the

priests and the people of these parishes to observe the good work of your sisters and their dedication to the Apostolate of Catholic Education both in the parochial schools and in the C.C.D. for the public school children. The people of both parishes have expressed their grateful appreciation of your sisters for their loving zeal for the progress of the children in Christian virtue and knowledge.[19]

Since the creation of the new Diocese of San Jose, your community no longer has a house in the new Archdiocese of San Francisco. I personally regret this because I have always admired the fine work your community has performed and above all your devoted community life.[20]

... Heartfelt expression of thanks for the exemplary service and witness of your sisters at Saint Cyprian's and Saint Simon's. Their work has been so fruitful for the entire church in the area. . . . [21]

It is evident that the members of the hierarchy in every geographical part of the country and in areas representing a variety of socio-economic levels are in agreement concerning the valuable role of religious in the field of Catholic education. They reflect, indeed, the sentiments of Pope Paul VI: "As we extol anew the value of this consecration, we recall a conviction of our predecessor Pius XII who used to say—we heard him often—that the strength of the Church of America was in the Catholic schools, and that the strength of the schools was in the religious—in their consecrated ecclesial love."[22]

In view of this strong support from the hierarchy, as well as the firm conviction of the sisters as evidenced by the fact that in a poll which preceded the 1981 chapter 95 percent[23] favored the retention of Catholic education as their apostolate, the capitulars unanimously affirmed this. Included in the constitutions submitted to the Sacred Congregation for approval was this statement which encapsulates the understanding of apostolic sanctity for the Sisters, Servants of the Immaculate Heart of Mary: "Since Catholic education is above all a matter of communicating Christ and of helping to form Christ in the lives of others, each sister, by the witness to Christ in her life and the joyful giving of her service, enters into the apostolic purpose of this Congregation. The sisters, through the ministry of Catholic Education, participate in this redemptive mission of the Church, especially in the Catholic schools."[24]

On April 26, 1983, approval was granted to these constitutions and this approbation marked an end to the period of experimentation. The Sacred Congregation expressed its appreciation for the work of the twelve preceding years, and the hope that *Faithful Witness* would indeed be the life-style for the congregation. In the words of Archbishop Mayer, "May the generous living of these constitutions encourage all the sisters of the institute to an ever deeper commitment to their consecrated life, to Christ and to the Church after the example of their founder, Father Gillet, and in the strong and loving spirit of Mary's Immaculate Heart."[25]

Chapter II

Origin of Witness: Charism and Early History

The early history of the Sisters, Servants of the Immaculate Heart of Mary has been recorded and well-documented by Mother Maria Alma, I.H.M.,[1] Sister M. Immaculata, I.H.M.,[2] and Sister M. Rosalita, I.H.M.[3] It is a fascinating story, marked by the cross, and in certain aspects, verifying that truth is sometimes stranger than fiction. For the reader who may not have immediate access to the works of the above-cited authors, a brief summary of the principal events is in order.

At a conference for Bishops and Major Religious Superiors in June 1983, Rev. John W. Padberg, S.J., speaking on the topic "Memory, Vision, and Structure: Historical Perspectives on the Experience of Religious Life in the Church," reminded his audience:

> In institutes founded for apostolic activities or charitable works, the members commit themselves to God in order to carry out this call to ministry that they have heard. It is not a question of two separate vocations; religious life and ministry. Historically, in fact,

the first thing to appear in the consciousness of founders or foundresses has often been an external need of the church and then, as a response to this need their call to a ministry . . . "to evangelize the poor" for a Vincentian, Redemptorist . . . "to Christianize education and educate the poor" for a Brother of the Christian Schools. . . . Each of these is not only the first thing which emerged in the consciousness of their founders, but rather it is what constitutes the central nucleus of the charism from which everything derives. . . . In these cases the service of God is centered on the ministry, and the religious life is born to further this ministry. All of these religious are "sanctified and sent" like Jesus (Jn. 10:36), that is to say, chosen by the Father and associated to the son in His redeeming work. They serve God by committing their lives and persons for the salvation of His sons and daughters. (Saint Thomas Aquinas, 2–2, q. 188 a.2)[4]

This was indeed the case in the founding of this congregation. A Belgian Redemptorist, Rev. Louis Florent Gillet,[5] who had volunteered in 1843 for missionary work in the United States, was assigned to assist Bishop Peter Paul LeFevre in the diocese of Detroit.[6] Having selected Monroe[7] as the site for a permanent foundation, Father served the French, German, and Irish Catholics within a radius of sixty miles north and west of this center.

Although he believed that the only way in which a vibrant group of committed Catholics could be formed was by ensuring that the children (especially the girls) would be firmly grounded in a knowledge of their faith and practices of devotion through education, in a Catholic school staffed[8] by religious women, he was unable to obtain any sisters. In a visit to Father Amadeus Rappe, Pastor of Toledo, and later Bishop of Cleveland, he learned that the pastor, a former chaplain of the Ursulines in Boulogne, France, was awaiting the arrival of three members of that community. Father Gillet frankly expressed his envy but ended by declaring, "Si je ne trouve pas des Religieuses, j'en fabriquerai."[9]

Working quietly, Father Gillet succeeded in interesting four women in his plan of founding a religious institute dedicated to the education of youth and on November 10, 1845, three of them came together in the little log cabin which served as the first convent. Therese Renault, the first to whom he had spoken of his dream when he was conducting a mission in Grosse Pointe, Michigan in 1843,[10] publicly received the habit of the new congregation on Sunday, December 14, 1845. The other two, Mary Maxis and Charlotte Schaaf,[11] former members of the Oblate Sisters of Providence whose vows had expired, had on November 30, 1845 privately received the habit and pronounced their vows according to the Rule drawn up by Father Gillet[12] and approved by Bishop LeFevre.[13] In religion these sisters were known as Sister Mary Celestine, Sister Mary Theresa and Sister Mary Ann, respectively. Sister Mary Theresa was named by Bishop LeFevre as first superior for a term of one year.[14] The name given to the congregation was Sisters of Providence.[15]

A school was opened on January 15, 1846 and attracted students in steadily increasing numbers.[16] Father Gillet was enjoying success and acclamation for his various undertakings in Michigan,[17] when a series of events involving calumny, misunderstanding, and litigation shattered his peace and that of the nascent community.[18] Although his innocence was promptly established, his superiors, deeming it prudent to remove him from Monroe at this time, recalled him to Baltimore on September 13, 1847.[19] There is no record after his departure of any correspondence with the members of the little community founded less than two years earlier.

On December 8, 1847[20] the decision was made to change the name of the community to Sisters, Servants of the Immaculate Heart of Mary, and to change the color of the habit from black to "sky blue."

During the first decade of its existence, the Immaculate Heart community had enjoyed a sense of security, stemming in no small part from the support of the Redemptorist Fathers who regarded the little sisterhood as part of their own apostolic effort since it was founded by one of their confreres and followed a rule based on their own. On May 1, 1855[21] the Redemptorists were withdrawn from Monroe, and the community was left without a permanent director for more than two years.

Ten years after its founding the community numbered twelve members, and in addition to the school at Monroe, the sisters taught in the newly formed German parish of Saint Michael's, Monroe, and in Saint Joseph's, Vienna (now Erie), Michigan.[22] Furthermore, during the summers, students from remote areas were received for a three-month session in order to be instructed and prepared for the Sacraments of Penance, Holy Eucharist, and Confirmation.[23]

Three years into the second decade, Bishop John Nepomucene Neumann[24] invited the community to staff a school in the Diocese of Philadelphia at Susquehanna, Pennsylvania and a series of events developed after the arrival of the sisters there, leading to an eventual separation of the community into two independent groups, one under the jurisdiction of the Bishop of Detroit, the other, the Bishop of Philadelphia. The last transfers from Detroit left the sisters in Michigan and Pennsylvania almost equally divided numerically.[25] Within the year, the twelve professed sisters in Pennsylvania were joined by twenty-two novices[26] and it is from this nucleus that the Immaculata congregation developed. In 1868 when the Diocese of Scranton was erected, the only two Catholic schools within its confines, Laurel Hill Academy and Saint John's Academy in Pittston, were both staffed by the Sisters, Servants of the Immaculate Heart of Mary. The founding Bishop (William O'Hara) wished to have a separate foundation for his diocese, and in August 1871 he advised the sisters of this. All twelve signified their complete willingness to place themselves under his jurisdiction,[27] although he indicated that any who wished might return to the Reading Motherhouse. Thus was formed the third autonomous group of the Sisters, Servants of the Immaculate Heart of Mary, with a motherhouse at Scranton, Pennsylvania.

The growth of the Immaculata community, which after this separation numbered sixty-one professed members, necessitated in the following year a transfer of the motherhouse from Reading to a larger building in West Chester,[28] and less than twenty years later a substantial addition was made event to that. The community continued to grow throughout the years, and on April 23, 1967 the present motherhouse at Immaculata was dedicated by Cardinal Krol.

In 1891 a great grace came to the community in a reunion with its founder, Rev. Louis Florent Gillet. As noted above, he left Monroe in 1847 and at that time requested dispensation from his vows as a Redemptorist. Early in 1848 his superiors gave him the option of returning to Europe or to Monroe, but withheld the dispensation.[29] There is a record of a second request,[30] which was reluctantly granted in 1850[31] and Father was received into the diocese of Cincinatti, carrying on his missionary labors in Darke and Shelby counties.[32] In 1853 the Redemptorist

Provincial, in a letter to Archbishop Hughes, remarked that he had learned of Father Gillet's reception into the Archdiocese of New York[33] but no records have been unearthed to date that give evidence of this. However, it is established that in early 1857[34] he was back in France, serving under Bishop de Garsignes as pastor of Bievres, with Cheret as its mission.

After a year and a half at that post he set out for South America by way of Africa, apparently never disembarking. By the end of this four-month journey he had reached the firm decision to reenter religious life,[35] this time in a contemplative order. Admitted[36] to the Cistercians of the Immaculate Conception at Senanque, France, August 22, 1858 he received the name Pere Marie Celestin.

Just as the small community of sisters to whom he said farewell in 1847 had by this time a new name and a different color habit, so also had he, the founder, undergone similar changes and these circumstances complicated efforts on either side to establish contact. The sisters had nothing to go on except a vague rumor that he had joined a Trappist group in Europe. Father had not made further inquiries because, as he states[37] in his account of the foundation, he had met a priest years before in Louvain who told him that there were indeed religious in Monroe but they were Sisters of the Heart of Mary. This response convinced him that his little community had died out.

Assigned as one of the group to establish a new community at Hautecombe in 1864,[38] Father spent the remaining years of his life in that community serving successively as Novice Master, Sub-Prior, and Prior.[39]

Meanwhile, on the other side of the Atlantic, in 1868 a former French Visitandine was admitted to the Sisters, Servants of the Immaculate Heart of Mary motherhouse at Reading, Pennsylvania and received the name, Sister Mary Clotilde.[40] Once, during her term as Mother Superior of the Visitation Convent at Moselle, France, she had journeyed to Ars to make her confession to the saintly Curé.[41] Although she mingled among a great throng of penitents and had in no way revealed her identity, he told her after her confession of the future dissolution of her community and her own eventual journey to America, where she would join a community dedicated to our lady and whose members wear a blue habit. Later, at the time of the dissolution of the community at Moselle, several Visitandines elected to join the Cisterciennes[42] and Sister Clotilde maintained a correspondence with one of them over the years.[43] Frequently in the letters she received, mention was made of Pere Celestin who served as chaplain to the nuns and whose sister was the Prioress, but never was there any thought that this Pere Celestin had been the founder of the congregation she had joined in America. Once by chance the name Gillet was mentioned,[44] and immediately Sister Clotilde initiated inquiries through her nephew, a Cistercian at the Motherhouse at Lerins,[45] to ascertain whether Pere Marie Celestin was indeed the Father Louis Florent Gillet, C.S.S.R. who forty-six years earlier had said, "Si je ne trouve pas des Religieuses, j'en fabriquerai." In commemoration of the forty-fifth anniversary of the founding, the sisters in Michigan had published in the *Michigan Catholic*[46] a brief account of the community along with sketches of the first log convent and Father Gillet; therefore a copy of this was submitted by Sister M. Clotilde to her nephew, who assured its safe delivery to Hautecombe. Pere Celestin, then nearing his seventy-ninth birthday, had the joy of learning that the tiny group of four religious whom he left in 1847 had increased a hundredfold, as young women consecrated their lives to God in one or another of the three distinct groups of Sisters, Servants of the Immaculate Heart of Mary.[47]

Because of his advanced age and physical infirmities,

the Founder was unable to visit his spiritual daughters, but he did write a short summary of the early years of the foundation.[48] Moreover, through the goodness of his confreres, copies of many of his conferences were made available.

Twenty-two months after the reunion on November 14, 1892,[49] Pere Celestin died and was buried among his brother Cistercians. However, in 1929, on the ninety-first anniversary of his ordination to the priesthood, his remains were brought back to Monroe through the diligent efforts of Mother Domitilla, Superior General at Monroe, Paul Claudel, and the Cistercians.[50] A recent publication with a summary of Pere Celestin's life by two Benedictine priests sheds added light on the exhumation process.[51]

In this period of Vatican II, in which religious are being urged to return to the spirit of their Founders,[52] the Sisters, Servants of the Immaculate Heart of Mary are singularly blessed in having in their possession rich documents in the very handwriting of their Founder, and ample testimony of his spirit in his treatises on the basic elements of the spiritual life. Part of this precious legacy includes conferences on prayer, humility, spiritual reading, charity, recollection, mortification, devotion to the Blessed Sacrament, to Our Lady, and to the Passion of Christ.[53] Moreover, as Vatican II calls religious to study the purpose for which a congregation was founded,[54] there is compelling evidence that the apostolate of the Catholic school was the operative motive in the founding of this congregation.

CHAPTER III

Extension of Witness: Apostolate

In the constitutions approved by the Sacred Congregation on April 26, 1983 the apostolate of the congregation is clearly affirmed: "The Sisters, through this ministry of Catholic education, partcipate in the redemptive mission of the Church, especially in Catholic Schools."

Periodic surveys of the members, especially in preparation for successive chapters during the period of experimentation, showed more than 95 percent of the sisters in favor of remaining in the apostolate which was the compelling reason for the founding of the congregation. Since the bishops assembled at Vatican II had declared: "As for Catholic parents, the Council calls to mind their duty to entrust their children to Catholic schools when and where this is possible,"[1] the need to maintain such schools was evident. In *Gaudim et Spes*, the truth is emphasized that men and women are indeed the crafters and molders of their community's culture and bear the responsibility to build a better world in truth and justice.[2] The Catholic school is the milieu par excellence in which principles can be inculcated and motivation provided to direct these future men and women in this tremendous work of shaping a culture and building a better world.

During the period 1966–1982 there has been a lamentable decline in the number of Catholic schools, but recent studies of the N.C.E.A. reveal that the trend may be being reversed.[3] Likewise, there has been a nationwide decline in the number of teaching religious. Sister Augusta Neal, basing her statistics on the *Catholic Directory*, points out that the 33,310 sisters engaged in teaching in 1982 represents a 65 percent decrease since 1966. She adds that there are also fewer schools in which to teach, citing a 28 percent decline in Catholic elementary schools and a 39 percent decline in secondary schools.[4]

Against this background, the history of the schools served by I.H.M.s during this period presents a striking contrast. The number of schools, on the elementary and secondary levels, each decreased by only one, leaving the grand total at 185. This figure includes the four instances in which schools were consolidated. In some schools waiting lists of students seeking admission are maintained, an evidence of the desire of parents to have their children educated in Catholic schools.

As pointed out by Sister Augusta Neal,[5] large numbers of the laity have responded to the invitations of Vatican II by coming forward to give service in the Church and it is through the work of zealous lay teachers who have collaborated with the sisters that these schools have continued to function in spite of the decrease in community membership. During the period mentioned, the Sisters, Servants of the Immaculate Heart of Mary responded to the appeals of bishops and pastors to staff schools in the dioceses of Raleigh, North Carolina, Atlanta, Georgia, Philadelphia, Pennsylvania, Richmond, Virginia, Harrisburg, Pennsylvania and Lincoln, Nebraska, all of which were in danger of closing because of withdrawal of their religious faculties.

The first school accepted was in the Diocese of Atlanta, Saint Joseph, Athens. The site of the present Saint Joseph's Church, purchased in 1873, had formerly housed the first Law School of the University of Georgia. Prior to that date, priests had come from Atlanta, Macon, and Augusta to care for the small flock of Catholics, celebrating Mass and administering the sacraments in their homes. Seventy-six years elapsed until the establishment of the first school on the first floor of the rectory by Reverend Walter Donovan in 1949. When new quarters became available as the enrollment grew, it was staffed by the Missionary Sisters of the Sacred Heart. However, early in 1969 the community informed Reverend Jarleth Burke, pastor, that the sisters currently staffing the school would be withdrawn in June.[6] An ad hoc committee made a pressing appeal to Immaculata, even submitting a tape recording of a public meeting in which parents and other parishioners pleaded for the continued operation of the school. As one parishioner later wrote: "It was not for the sake of educational excellence that we so desperately wanted to keep our school open—our main concern was for the faith of our children. In addition to this primary task of nurturing the faith of the Catholic children, the sisters have a significant missionary opportunity with the non-Catholic children in the school."[7]

Even though the congregation had not planned to accept any additional schools, the situation of these Catholics in this university area seemed exceptional and so Mother Claudia, superior general of the congregation, and the members of the council acquiesced, informing the pastor on April 23, 1969 of the decision to send sisters in August of that year. On September 2, the founding community, Mother Thomas Bernard Volpe, Sister Anne David Smith, and Sister M. Judith Anne Kreipe welcomed 226 pupils, and the school threatened with extinction carried on. There has been a slow but gradual growth in enrollment, reaching a 16 percent increase in 1983, and on November 2, ground was broken for a new school.

The new facility was dedicated by Bishop Thomas Donnellen on October 21, 1984. In addition to the physical expansion, there has also been academic growth. The school, long accredited by the state of Georgia, applied for admission to the Southern Association of Schools and Colleges and was accepted as an official candidate six weeks after the dedication ceremony.[8]

The second school accepted in 1969 was Saint Mary's, Norfolk, Virginia, staffed by the Daughters of Wisdom since 1940. When the prospect of their withdrawal and the distinct possibility of the school closing arose, Bishop Russell invited the community to accept a role in staffing the first intercommunity elementary school in the Richmond diocese. St. Mary's, an inner-city school, with an enrollment of 275, 5 of whom were white and 110 were non-Catholics, had a program from kindergarten through eighth grade. Considering this a unique situation, Mother Claudia and the council accepted the Bishop's invitation[9] and named Sister Robert Miriam Adamski principal, and Sister Maureen Agnes Eggert as seventh grade teacher to join with Sister Robert, D.W., and Sister Jerome, O.S.F., in the effort to maintain the school when three Daughters of Wisdom would be withdrawn in June. The Sisters of I.H.M. resided in St. Gregory the Great Convent, Virginia Beach and commuted to Norfolk until September 1971, at St. Pius X in Norfolk from 1971 to 1973, and at Star of the Sea, Virginia Beach thereafter.

The communities that had agreed to experiment in

the intercommunity school gradually found it necessary to withdraw their sisters, the Franciscan Sisters of Mill Hill, after the first year, and the Daughters of Wisdom after the third. From 1972 the Sisters of I.H.M. continued with seven lay women, until 1975, when a Sister of St. Anne joined the faculty.

In March 1977 the pastor Father Thomas J. Quinlan appealed to Mother Claudia for additional staff, praising the work of the I.H.M.s.[10] It was with sincere regret that Mother was compelled to reply in the negative, and that in June of 1978 the sisters were withdrawn. However, their service in the critical years enabled the school to survive, and later to be consolidated with a school staffed by the Sisters of Notre Dame.

In 1971 the community responded to the urgent request to preserve another school that was in danger of closing, Saint Eleanor's, Collegeville, Pennsylvania. This parish, established in 1911, took care of Catholics in a section of Montgomery county who had, since 1880, been ministered to only by Jesuit missionaries on occasional visits from Bally, and later by priests from Saint Mary's, Phoenixville and Saint Aloysius in Pottstown. A parish school, conducted by the Sisters of Notre Dame de Namur was opened in the convent in 1943 and moved to a modern school building in 1948. When the Sisters of Notre Dame found it necessary to withdraw in June 1971, an appeal was made to the I.H.M.s. On March 11, 1971 Mother Claudia wrote to Msgr. Francis B. Schulte (later Bishop Schulte), explaining why they could not assume this responsibility[11] but, in view of the fact that the children attending school could not possibly receive a Catholic education if it was closed, the congregation reversed its decision and agreed to send a sister principal in 1971. Sister Eleanor Mary Knipper, assisted by a lay staff, welcomed 203 students in September.

While Sister commuted from Bishop Kenrick faculty house in Norristown during this year, plans were made to reopen the convent and have additional sisters collaborate in the work of the parish. On June 25, 1972 a summer session for religious instruction was opened and in August the community for 1972–73 assembled, including Sister M. Augusta Tallon, superior and director of religious education, Sister Eleanor Mary Knipper, principal, Sister Maria Novatus Curnan, secretary, Sister M. Eucharista Mullin, tutor, and Sister St. Brendan O'Brien, housekeeper. In addition to the students in the school, 146 students, grades seven through twelve registered for evening C.C.D. classes.

Although there was a decrease in the enrollment in September 1972, possibly because of the uncertainty regarding the continuation of the school, once the convent was established and religious personnel added, the school had experienced a phenomanal growth of 54 percent by 1985.[12]

When Bishop Vincent Waters appealed in December 1972 for sisters to staff Sacred Heart Cathedral School in Raleigh, North Carolina, the situation also seemed to be one that demanded special consideration and a deviation from the policy of refusing new schools. This inner-city school of two hundred pupils had been in existence since 1909 and, through the zealous work of the Dominican sisters of Caldwell, New Jersey had served a missionary purpose in this area in which only 1 percent of the population was Catholic. Reverend Robert Lawson, superintendent, of schools, visited Villa Maria and pleaded eloquently for assistance "to save the school" when the Dominican sisters notified the pastor of their withdrawal, effective June 1973. The plea did not go unheard and, responding to this call which had such a missionary aspect to it, Mother Claudia assigned the pioneer community: S. Bernard Marie

Sullivan, S. Mary Genevieve Brennan, S. Theresa Celine Duffy, S. Mary Angele Alpigini.

It brought joy to the heart of Bishop Waters when the sisters arrived to open the convent August 14, 1973 and the school continued in existence with 206 students enrolled in September. In addition to teaching religion in the school, Sister Mary Angele enrolled as a candidate for a master's degree in sociology at nearby State University of North Carolina, and completed requirements for that degree in 1976.

In 1984, when the school celebrated its seventy-fifth anniversary, Gov. James B. Hunt honored the school by a personal visit during Catholic Schools Week.

The next call for assistance came from the Saint Peter Claver parish in Philadelphia. Saint Peter Claver Church, dedicated by Archbishop Ryan on January 3, 1892, was the first of the churches established in Philadelphia dedicated to the cause of the blacks, a segment of the Catholic population in which the Archbishop took a deep spiritual interest. During that year the boys' school was conducted in the basement of the church with Brother Celsus, C.S.Sp. and the Sisters of the I.H.M. in charge, while the Sisters of Notre Dame de Namur taught the girls. In 1906, through the arduous efforts of Rev. Christopher J. Plunkett, C.S.Sp. a sufficient sum of money was collected to build a school, a large granite structure on Lombard Street. By this time, Mother Katharine Drexel had established the Sisters of the Blessed Sacrament, with the education of negroes as a special apostolate[13] and members of that congregation took over the boys' school, while the Sisters of Notre Dame de Namur continued to teach the girls.

In June 1947, the total enrollment of Saint Peter Claver School was 232, and in September of that year the Blessed Sacrament Sisters took the combined group of boys and girls, and the Sisters of Notre Dame de Namur concluded their fifty-five years of devoted service in this segment of the Lord's vineyard. In September 1971, however, that community informed the pastor, Rev. Leonard Trotter, C.S.Sp. that they would be unable to supply sisters for the next school year. Mother Alice Anita, S.S.J. agreed to assign four sisters from nearby Saint Teresa's School, which was being closed by the archdiocese that year, for a one-year interim period until an effort could be made to form an intercommunity faculty in 1973.

In March 1973[14] Monsignor Schulte requested that one I.H.M. sister be part of that faculty and since the congregation was so concerned about minority groups and so eager to improve educational opportunities for them, Monsignor Schulte's invitation was gladly accepted. In September 1973 Sister Miriam Thomas Callahan, as eighth grade teacher, joined Sister Francis Paula Forde, S.S.J., principal, Sister Eleanor McFadden, S.S.J., Sister Michael Ann, S.H.F.N, and Sister Barbara Hoffman, S.M. on the first faculty.

At that time the enrollment was 250 in grades one through eight, but this declined steadily in each succeeding year. Gradually each of the communities involved withdrew: the Sisters of the Holy Family in 1974, the Sisters of I.H.M. in 1977, and the Sisters of Saint Joseph in 1982. A lay principal was named in September 1982 and one Mercy Sister remained for that scholastic year.

The Holy Ghost Fathers, who minister to the parish, were finally forced to close the school because of a combination of factors: the financial burden of the lay teachers' salaries, the need for extensive repairs to the plant, and the decline in enrollment. In the final year of its existence the enrollment was less than one hundred with more than 50 percent non-Catholic. Moreover, many of these students did not reside within the immediate area of the school, but traveled there from neighborhoods where a Catholic education was available to them.

From the Midwest early in 1981 came a request from Bishop Glennon Flavin to send sisters to Lincoln, Nebraska, to staff a school which was being left by the sisters of the Blessed Virgin Mary after ninety-one years of fruitful service. Saint Mary's, an inner-city school with an enrollment of three hundred students, in the Old Cathedral parish was the first parochial school in Lincoln and the oldest Catholic school still in existence in that city. It has been preceded only by an academy operated by the Sisters of the Holy Child Jesus of Rosemont, Pennsylvania, from 1883 till 1907. With high academic standards, the academy blazed a trail of excellence in Catholic education which Saint Mary's and subsequent schools emulated. It is significant that within the last decade enrollment in Catholic schools in this diocese has increased, running counter to the national trends. The Sisters, Servants of the Immaculate Heart of Mary accepted this school and Sister Jude Mary O'Donnell became principal in 1981. Even in the short span of time since then, it has become evident that high standards are characteristic of the school, since students have attained awards both in diocesan competitions and in those sponsored by the city for both public and nonpublic schools.[15]

Another school within the Archdiocese of Philadelphia which received notification of withdrawal of religious faculty, was Saint Lucy School, Manayunk, staffed by the Sisters of the Holy Child Jesus from its inception in 1956 until 1976. This year marked the fiftieth anniversary of this parish which consisted of Italian Catholics who desperately wished their school to continue. At the request of Monsignor Schulte, Mother Claudia agreed to assign a principal, Sister Doloretta Maria Rooney and an assistant principal, Sister Jane Marie Diamond. In September 1976, the school opened with an enrollment of 211 and with 5 lay women and 2 men serving on the faculty. The sisters resided at Saint John's Convent, Manayunk.

In 1979 the pastor, Reverend Michael A. Capuano wrote to Mother Claudia,[16] praising the leadership of the sisters and requesting an addition to the Saint Lucy faculty. It was impossible to accede to that request, and although the community continued to serve these students, on March 6, 1984, Mother Marie Genevieve found it necessary to inform the pastor that the sisters would not return in September. A lay principal has been appointed.

Another school which was suffering from imminent withdrawal of its religious faculty in 1979 was Our Lady of the Sacred Heart, Hilltown, Pennsylvania. Since the I.H.M.s staffed the school of the adjoining parish an appeal was made to Immaculata when the Mission Workers of the Sacred Heart could no longer remain in the school. In order to enable the students enrolled to continue their Catholic education an agreement was made to consolidate Saint Agnes School, Sellersville and Our Lady of the Sacred Heart School, Hilltown with Sister Mary Eileen Turner, principal, Sister Ellen Thomas Ertel, Sister Miriam Teresa Madden, and six lay teachers. Grades one through three would utilize the Sellersville, and four through eight the Hilltown building.

At the time of the decision the combined enrollment of the two schools was 240, and as of 1986 it is 265. Once more, this time in a rural area of Bucks County, through the action of the I.H.M.s Catholic parents were assured the opportunity of keeping their children in a Catholic school as the Bishops of Vatican II had urged.

The parish of Our Lady of the Sacred Heart, Hilltown

had been established in 1911, and by 1927, the pastor, Reverend John N. Wachter, with the aid of the zealous parishioners, had succeeded in having a parochial school. In the ensuing years the parish faithfully supported the school even during years when the enrollment dropped below one hundred. Like their predecessors of fifty-two years earlier, in 1979 the pastor, Reverend Charles Dombay, and the parishioners exerted every effort in the cause of Catholic education. The consolidation not only attained the result of providing Catholic education for a segment of the children who would otherwise be deprived of it, but because of the increased enrollment[17] in each grade, a stronger program was developed which also benefited the students in the Sellersville area.

The next school accepted during this period presents a sharp contrast to Our Lady of the Sacred Heart School. Almost three times the size, it is located in a prosperous suburban area, Miami Shores in Florida. For many years the superintendent of schools had been anxious for the community to accept other elementary schools in the rapidly developing Archdiocese of Miami, in which the sisters have staffed Epiphany School since 1953. At that time, the superintendent of schools, Reverend William McKeever, in appealing for sisters, had pointed out that during the past few years southern Florida had experienced an unprecedented growth, and that in many areas the Catholic population had tripled. As he expressed it: " . . . we rejoice in the knowledge that we are now presented with the golden opportunity of reclaiming this part of the Southland for Christ and His Church. But we must act now—delay or vacillation will certainly mean a repetition of the past losses the Church experienced in the South."[18] In addition to their work in Epiphany, the sisters staffed two secondary schools, Notre Dame Academy since 1959 and Our Lady of Lourdes Academy, founded in 1963.

In 1981, however, the constantly declining enrollment at Notre Dame Academy, due principally to a changing neighborhood that parents considered unsafe for their daughters and that the diocese viewed as crime-ridden, led to the decision to condolidate with Curley High School in a more desirable location. This school, originally an all boys' school, had become coeducational. An agreement was reached for two Immaculate Heart Sisters formerly at Notre Dame to teach in the consolidated school[19] and for the congregation to accept the parochial school in the parish of Saint Rose of Lima, Miami Shores, previously staffed by Dominican Sisters of Adrian, Michigan, who planned to withdraw in June 1981.

The convent opened on August 14, 1981, with the following community: Sister Anthony Miriam DeCarlo, superior, Notre Dame-Curley Faculty; Sister Ann Bernard Gradl, principal; Sister Rosaria Unger, grade eight; Sister Marcella Cloran, tutor; Sister Daniel Mary Smyth, director of learning center; Sister Mary of the Infant Canavan, Notre Dame-Curley Faculty. In September, 1981, 515 students were welcomed by the faculty which included also Sister Rose Bernadette, O.P., and sixteen lay teachers.

As in many areas of Florida a sizable influx of Cuban students and of other national groups was experienced at Saint Rose School. The administration and faculty made a concerted effort to inculcate in the students a respect for the various cultures and their traditions. Their success in this, as well as in fostering academic excellence, has led to an award to be presented by the United States government. In the national elementary school recognition program, Saint Rose School was visited by a committee of educators who acclaimed it as deserving of the award. President

Reagan and Secretary of Education Bennett will receive the principals of the schools so honored.

In the period under consideration, 1966–82, as Sister Augusta Neal S.N.D. noted[20] the trend was the closing of schools, so it is noteworthy that in addition to "saving" schools already established, the sisters accepted the challenge of opening two new schools. The first of these was Saint Ephrem's, in the rapidly growing area of Bensalem, Bucks County, Pennsylvania, a parish established in June 1966. In 1969 the Archdiocese of Philadelphia, after analysis of statistics, determined that a school should be built in that parish and be established as the first interparochial school of the archdiocese,[21] serving both Saint Ephrem's parishioners and those of nearby Saint Mark's Bristol. The school in Bristol, one of the earliest founded in the diocese, dated back to January 1888, and was inadequate for the size of the student body and inconvenient in many respects. Forseeing decline both in the numbers of teaching religious and in the student population the authorities believed that the Catholics would be better served by interparochial institutions. The school opened in September 1969 with 549 students. Meanwhile, the parishioners at Saint Mark's still desired their own school, and when the unoccupied building was ravaged by fire in 1970,[22] they set out to provide suitable quarters. In September 1971 the school was reopened for grades one through three of Saint Mark's children and by 1977 for the remaining grades. Saint Ephrem school as a separate entity now has an enrollment 15 percent higher than the total interparochial enrollment of 1969, and the combined population of the two schools is currently 41 percent higher than the 1969 figure.[23] The sisters continue to staff both schools, mindful of the words of Pope John Paul II, " . . . institutes are called to continue to foster, in dynamic faithfulness, those corporate commitments which were related to the original charism, which were authenticated by the Church and which still fulfill important needs of the People of God."

The Holy Father further declared that the Catholic school system, invaluable for the Church in the United States, was an excellent means "for permeating the entire community with Christ's trust and love. It is one of the apostolates in which women religious have made and are still making an incomparable contribution."[24]

Lincoln, Nebraska, was the site in which another new school was begun in 1979. The community responded to the request of Bishop Flavin to serve in the newly established parish of Saint Joseph's in the southeastern section of the city. A school had been constructed and plans made to commence with kindergarten and grades one through three in September 1979. At the Philadelphia airport on August 24 more than one hundred sisters and relatives gathered to say good-bye to the pioneers, Sister Joseph Fidelis Dorwart, Sister Lorraine Holzman, and Sister John Evelyn DiTrolio. When they had embarked, one of the stewardesses remarked to them, "It must be a great feeling to have your whole church behind you." As the sisters later confessed, they needed this reassurance, for the parents in the area not knowing the sisters and not having had the experience of having children in Catholic schools, did not demonstrate great alacrity in enrolling their sons and daughters. On opening day sixty-three students reported, and from this modest nucleus a thriving school has developed, an evidence of the parents' appreciation of the high educational standards maintained. Within five years the enrollment increased by 353 percent, and it was necessary to erect a twenty-two thousand foot addition to the existing facilities.[25]

In this vibrant Catholic community, there is perpetual adoration of the Blessed Sacrament, and in 1981 the latest endeavor to involve parishioners resulted in the establishment of a "Prayer Line." The purpose was to develop a spiritual union among the parishioners and to serve those in need. When a request is phoned in to a number listed weekly in the parish bulletin it is relayed to more than thirty persons who join in praying for the intention of the caller. For older members of the parish this apostolate has been especially meaningful since, even though they cannot leave their homes, they have the satisfaction of making a valuable contribution through their prayers.

In addition to the sisters' activities recounted above in opening new schools and in staffing established schools in areas where other religious were being withdrawn, this period led to a third phenomenon, the consolidation of schools in sections where enrollment was declining. Bishop George Guilfoyle of Camden, New Jersey, in 1968 drew up a plan to consolidate facilities in Cape May County to improve the educational milieu of the students. This involved the decision to close Saint Paul's school in Stone Harbor. In a letter to Mother Maria Pacis he stated that by eliminating double grades and providing single grades one through eight, he believed that the educational opportunities would be enhanced and that the parishioners would willingly endure the inconveniences occasioned by having to provide transportation for their children.[26]

The Diocese of Allentown, in which many towns had sprung up with coal mining as the principal industry, had experienced a heavy population loss since the 1940s. In an effort to continue to provide quality education to the Catholic children, the Office of Education initiated a lengthy study of population projections, of existing facilities, and of available religious teachers and drew up a consolidation plan which involved several schools staffed by the I.H.M.s.

For example, Ashland and Girardville, approximately fifteen miles apart, had four Catholic schools, each serving fewer than two hundred students. Saint Mauritius School in Ashland has been staffed by the Sisters of Saint Francis, Glen Riddle, who had announced their intention to withdraw in June 1970. Monsignor Alfred Barrett, therefore, suggested that the Sisters of Jesus Crucified who were presently at Saint Vincent's, Girardville take over an I.H.M. school, Saint Joseph School, Frackville, and that a consolidated school, Immaculate Heart Elementary School, be established to serve the students from Ashland and Girardville. The building in Saint Joseph parish, Ashland would house grades one through six and that in Girardville, grades one, two, three, seven and eight, thus obviating the need for any students in grades one through three to be bussed. Six Sisters of the I.H.M., assisted by lay teachers, would constitute the faculty. By this arrangement, only two school buildings and two convents would be utilized, and this would ease the financial burden of the pastors in these struggling parishes.[27]

Any suggestion that the schools might be closed greatly distressed these parishioners, for the school was a greatly valued part of the parish for which many sacrifices had been made down through the years. For example, Saint Joseph's Girardville parish came into being August 10, 1870,[28] during the most violent period of local history, the beginning of the labor movement and the Molly Maguires. Fifty years elapsed before a school could be provided, and even during its construction tragedy ensued when a violent storm blew down the frame, killing the foreman.[29] By 1924,[30] however, the school included both elementary and high school grades, the latter fully accredited by the Department of Public Instruction in Harrisburg.

It is interesting to note that both Dennis Cardinal

Dougherty, former Archbishop of Philadelphia and Most Rev. Joseph Daley, former Bishop of Harrisburg were from this area. Cardinal Dougherty was born in Homesville, which was part of the parish of Saint Joseph, Ashland and he was educated in the public schools of Girardville, as there were no parochial schools available. Later, as chief shepherd of the Archdiocese of Philadelphia, he asserted that his great concern for providing Catholic education stemmed from the fact that he had not enjoyed that privilege himself.

The plan proposed by Monsignor Barrett was approved and in September 1972 the Immaculate Heart Elementary School came into being[31] with Sister Grace Regina Brereton, principal, and the following faculty: Sister Alma Dolores Lavelle, Sister Benedict Joseph Komly, Sister Helene Thomas Connolly, Sister Incarnata Maria DiPilla, Sister Maria Josina Paladine, Sister Rose Julie Barry, Sister Vincent Patrice Nally, Barbara Eiche, David Fennelly, and William Schappell. Sister Mary Cecilia Ashnalt taught music, and Sister Marie Carmel Powers and Sister Mary Conrad Homyak served as tutors.

During the ensuing years, other changes came about because of fluctuations in enrollment, and by 1979 the arrangement became K–4 at Saint Joseph, Ashland and 5–8 at Saint Joseph, Girardville with the entire religious faculty residing in Ashland. By 1981, since both school buildings, over sixty years old, required extensive repairs, it was decided to modernize the Girardville facility and base the entire student body there. During the years, the parents of children in five parishes have had the chance to provide Catholic education for their sons and daughters. When the necessity arose of contributing funds for the refurbishing of the building in Girardville, a letter from a grateful parent appeared in the local paper, ending with the words: "May I add that because our school is run down, our Catholic education is not. My children have always been taught well by the I.H.M.s. The love and understanding given them cannot be replaced by all the fringes in the world."[32]

On November 19, 1976, representatives from the Philadelphia Archdiocesan School Office and from the I.H.M. community met with the pastors and principals of Saint Veronica's and Our Lady of Pompeii parishes to present a plan for consolidation of the schools. The latter, located within the geographic boundaries of the former parish, had been established in 1929,[33] in response to a request from Cardinal Dougherty to take care of Italian immigrants lest they would be proselytized by other sects. Now, fifty years later, the grandchildren of these earlier immigrants could well be incorporated into the student body at Saint Veronica's and the educational opportunities would be greater since the low enrollment (141 in 8 grades) had necessitated double grades in Our Lady of Pompeii school. Both buildings could be utilized, which would permit learning centers to be established and library facilities to be enlarged.

The parents, however, had a strong desire to maintain the school and after several meetings with the authorities voted to keep the school open with an entire lay faculty.[34] After three years of operation it was not found feasible to continue, and in 1980 the building became an annex to Saint Veronica's school as originally recommended.

In view of the parents' opposition to the consolidation and the intermingling of the students from the two schools, a glimpse into history offers an interesting episode. When Our Lady of Pompeii school was seriously damaged by fire in 1940 the educational program was not interrupted, since the children from grades one through six were accommodated in the corresponding grades of Saint Veronica's while the seventh and eighth grades were taught in the church basement during the six month period of rebuilding![35]

In another section of the Archdiocese of Philadelphia a similar situation existed, since in Bridgeport there were two Catholic schools one city block apart, both staffed by Sisters of I.H.M. Within the geographic boundaries of Saint Augustine Parish, the parish Our Lady of Mount Carmel had served the Italians of that area since 1924, with the school established in 1952. On December 9, 1976 plans to consolidate the schools were proposed and in September 1977, Saint Augustine-Our Lady of Mount Carmel School began to function.[36] Both buildings continued to be used, but as a result of the consolidation, the educational program has been improved and space has been more effectively utilized in providing such facilities as a computer laboratory and improved library quarters. The convent of Our Lady of Mount Carmel was closed in August 1979, and the religious faculty has resided in the Saint Augustine facility. In addition to the economic advantages of this arrangement for the parish, the community life of the sisters had been enhanced.

In the Archdiocese of Philadelphia, plans were made to consolidate schools, not with the intent of closing any but for the purpose of improving the instructional program. For example, in Coatesville[37] three schools were in operation, each with an enrollment of less than two hundred, which necessitated double grades. Therefore, a plan was devised whereby all the schools would remain open, with specific grades housed in each building, one principal charged with the administration, and the three pastors sharing the financial burden. It was also possible to close Saint Joseph convent since the Immaculate Heart Sisters could reside at Saint Cecilia's. The Bernardine Sisters continued to reside at Saint Stanislaus. As a result of these adjustments, the instructional program was improved, facilities became available for learning centers and library, personnel was reduced, and the community life of the sisters improved.

Some schools were indeed closed during this period, but only in cases where it was established that the pupils they served had access to Catholic education in another institution. The first of these, Our Lady of Angels, had been established in 1925 to take care of children of Italian parentage residing in the West Philadelphia area. The original enrollment of 450 children had far exceeded the expectations of Reverend Victor Strumia, pastor, and the sisters assigned to open the school, which was located within the geographic boundaries of Saint Gregory's parish. Although it flourished for most of its fifty years of existence, by the late sixties and early seventies declining enrollment signified that the need for this type of school was not so urgent as it had been at the time of its establishment. By June 1973, with the total enrollment under two hundred, only six students were seeking admission to first grade, and therefore, the following year, Bishop Lohmuller announced that the school would be closed in June 1975.[38] Arrangements had been made for students to be accepted in Saint Gregory's school, Our Mother of Sorrows school, and Saint Donato's.

Declining enrollment also dictated the closing of Saint Gertrude School, West Conshohocken, in 1977,[39] since the children could transfer to either Saint Matthew, Saint Mary or Saint Cosmas and Damien School in Conshohocken. As a result, three sisters would be freed to continue the apostolate in schools where the need was greater. This marked the beginning of a series of studies as to how the community could best serve the cause of Catholic education in face of declining religious personnel.

It is important to note that one piece of legislation that had a significant impact on Catholic elementary schools was the Pennsylvania School Bus Law, which became operative, after much controversy, in 1965.[40] Under its provisions, children attending nonpublic school are transported to their schools within school districts and along established bus routes. Therefore, in many cases parents could send their children to classes in nearby parishes, a situation which did not exist at the time these separate, small schools had been established.

In upstate Pennsylvania, the city of Jim Thorpe had two Catholic schools in operation in 1979, with a combined population of 371. Since the Immaculate Conception School building was a concern structurally even though it had been well maintained through the years and since its ninety-four students could be provided for in nearby Saint Joseph School conducted by the Sisters of Christian Charity, the community petitioned the authorities to sanction the closing of the former. The pastors of the two parishes agreed, and Dr. James Cusimano, Superintendent of Schools for the Diocese of Allentown, made the announcement April 29, 1980[41] that in September all children would be welcome in Saint Joseph School.

Saint Nicholas School, Weatherly, was another of the schools in the coal regions which could not survive the steep decline in enrollment, for in its last year of operation only eighty-seven pupils attended in all eight grades. As the Catholic schools in McAdoo could easily admit them, the school was closed in 1981.[42]

In Centralia, noxious fumes from underground fires in the defunct mines caused government officials to relocate the inhabitants. School authorities had been advised of the danger in 1977 and regretfully began planning to close the school. As in the other cases cited, Catholic education was available in nearby Holy Spirit Schools, Mount

Carmel for members of these families which were awaiting relocation when Saint Ignatius School closed in 1981. During the eighty-two years of its existence this school had been blessed with an exceptionally high number of religious vocations, counting seventeen priests and forty-five sisters among its graduates.

The final school closing in the period being studied was Saint Rose of Lima, Eddystone. Founded in 1916 both the school and the convent facilities had been deteriorating while student enrollment had been declining especially after the closing of the Westinghouse plant in nearby Lester. Saint Madeline school in Ridley Park was accessible to the students and had space to accommodate them, so Msgr. Schulte began initial negotiations in March, 1980,[43] which resulted in a merger of the two student bodies at the Ridley Park school in September 1981. The pastors of the two parishes reached agreement regarding fiscal concerns and the school is now known as Saint Madeleine-Saint Rose elementary school.

On the secondary level, in addition to Notre Dame High School mentioned above, the congregation, after serious study, withdrew from Norfolk Catholic High School, Norfolk Virginia in 1975. An invitation to serve on the intercommunity faculty of Bishop Hafey High School in Hazleton, Pennsylvania was accepted, and in 1976 Sister Regina Anthony Kane and Sister Mary Paraclete Flaig became the pioneers in this first apostolic endeavor of the congregation in the diocese of Scranton. After nine years of happy and fruitful service, decline in personnel made it necessary to withdraw in June 1985.

In the interest of completeness, another case of the community withdrawing is included here, although it too was subsequent to the date used in Sister Augusta Neal's study.[44] The school in Saint Madeleine Sophie's parish,

Philadelphia, resembled in many respects that of Saint Peter Claver, with a high percentage of students who did not reside within the geographical boundaries of the parish and who could attend Catholic schools in their own locality. For this reason, when declining membership in the Sisters, Servants of the Immaculate Heart community caused the authorities to try to ascertain where their service was most essential, this school was targeted as one from which they should withdraw in 1984. However, in spite of this, the priests and parents chose to keep the school in operation with lay personnel.[45]

As noted above,[46] the sisters in addition to their schools in North America also serve in Peru and Chile, and as the decade of the sixties opened, they operated five schools in Latin America in which approximately four thousand students were enrolled.[47] Four of these were in Peru where the first, Villa Maria Academy, had been founded March 15, 1923 at the request of Monsignor Emilio Lisson, C.M., who, as Archbishop of Lima, was aware of the need for up-to-date schools, conducted in English by teaching religious. Since the Peruvian government at that time was promoting the establishment of home industries, a knowledge of English was a great asset, hence the teaching of it became an entering wedge for proselytizing groups in this country which according to its constitution professed the Roman Catholic religion.

Villa Maria Academy, which enrolled girls from first grade through high school, chartered by the Peruvian Board of Education, and later approved by the Southern Association of Colleges and Secondary Schools, had a curriculum closely resembling that of the schools in the United States. All instruction was given in English except for Peruvian history and geography, which according to national law are required to be taught in Spanish by native teachers.

As the first school established in Peru by a religious congregation from the United States, it has flourished since its inception and through its hundreds of graduates has had a significant effect on Peruvian life. In 1965 the high school division moved from Miraflores to a new facility in La Planicie, a suburb of Lima.

The first parochial school in Peru, San Antonio in the seaport town of Callao, was opened in 1928 and placed under the direction of the Sisters, Servants of the Immaculate Heart of Mary. Destroyed in the earthquake of 1940,[48] the original building was promptly replaced and enlarged. The scope of this present work does not permit a detailed account of the accomplishments of these two schools, except to indicate that they had a significant effect on the social history of Lima. The pupils in Callao came from homes of dire poverty and their parents had not enjoyed the privilege of an education. San Antonio school provided them not only with elementary education but through its efficient commercial high school equipped them with marketable skills which gave them entreé to the emerging industries mentioned above. As bilingual secretaries, the graduates were in great demand. Moreover, the sisters established there the same high standards of moral training and of preparation for gracious living which characterized the academy attended by the upper class families, and thus inculculated a proper self-esteem in their graduates. In the academy, the sisters earnestly strove to develop in the young people a realization of their responsibility in regard to sharing their material goods with those less fortunate. Thus by training the impoverished and raising the consciousness of the wealthy the sisters did much to effect the emergence of a middle class hitherto nonexistent in that area. In 1960 the enrollment at Villa Maria was 1,275, and at San Antonio, 884.

When the Marianist Brothers and Fathers from Dayton, Ohio, came to Peru to fulfill a great need by establishing a school for boys and thus to strengthen the faith of the future leaders of the country, they sought the coopertion of the sisters in 1944, requesting that they assume the task of teaching the students in their early grades.[49] Thus Escuela Immaculado Corazon was founded, consisting of kindergarten through grade three. The number of applicants was so large that it immediately became evident that the rented facilities were inadequate so, within a year, additional ground was purchased and the present imposing structure was erected. Mother Maria Pacis, the first superior and principal exerted her uncommon qualities of leadership, and as a result, seeds of faith and scholarship were planted in these boys during these crucial formative years. As the Bishops of Vatican II twenty years later expressed it in their document on the missions: "Brothers and nuns, likewise, play an indispensable role in planting and strengthening the kingdom of Christ in souls, and in the work of further extending it, both by their prayers and active work."[50]

In Chile, Villa Maria Academy for girls had been established in Santiago in 1940 at the request of Archbishop Aldo Laghi, the Papal Nuncio in Chile who had become familiar with Villa Maria in Lima and with the Sisters of the Immaculate Heart during the years in which he had served as Papal Nuncio in Peru. Patterned on its sister school to the north, Villa Maria served girls from kindergarten through high school with English as the principal language used for instruction.[51]

When, in 1944, the United States Department of State created a Division of Cultural Relations with the objective of developing a more effective rapport between United States and other American Republics, the sisters, because of their contribution to this development, were invited by Secretary of State Cordell Hull to participate in a conference held in Washington, D.C. November 10, 1945. Thus, on the hundredth anniversary of the founding of the congregation, the sisters, who had been styled by some Latin Americans "the most effective goodwill ambassadors to Latin America,"[52] joined with federal officials to discuss the furthering of their work in Peru and Chile. As noted above,[53] the founder of the congregation had once set out for South America but never settled there. His spiritual daughters may be responding to that call through their labors a century later.

In 1955, Reverend Nevin Hayes, O.Carm.,[54] (now Bishop Hayes) appealed to the congregation to staff a parish school in the district of San Antonio south of Miraflores in Peru. The school Nuestra Senora del Carmen was planned by the pastor to commence with kindergarten and grades one through three for boys only, with the intent of adding a grade each year, then extending it to girls and eventually adding a high school. The community accepted the invitation, and the school developed as projected. The present student body, numbering 1,041 in grades one through six (the group taught by the sisters), includes many children of men and women who were former students in Callao.

As the Congregation was preparing to mark the twentieth anniversary of the foundation in Chile, Reverend Francis Provenzano, C.S.C. requested that the sisters staff a school in Las Condes which was being established to provide education for the very poor children who lived in the poblaciones there. Father had written: "We ask you to assign two sisters to take over the school, for we are convinced that they alone can conduct a good, thoroughly Catholic school. . . . The combined efforts of our two communities in the work of Escuela de San Francisco can be a worthy effort to help the underprivileged for the greater honor and glory of God."[55]

Since the spirit of the congregation in imitation of Saint Alphonsus is to show special love for the poor, the invitation was warmly welcomed and in January 1961 Sister Marie Edwardine Leonard and Sister Ana Luisa Downey began the school which would change the lives of these impoverished boys and their parents. Located in the Andes foothills of suburban Santiago, it was a barrio school for campesinos, children of the tillers of the soil, who were perfectly satisfied to remain illiterate. Neither the children nor the parents were interested in education, a privilege of which they considered themselves unworthy. In their first year of teaching there, the sisters had forty children in grades one and two. The Holy Cross Fathers were responsible for the fiscal management of the school, which received government aid for maintenance and teachers' salaries, and consequently was subject to government inspection with oral examination of students.[56] By 1966, the school had reached the full complement of grades K–8, with an enrollment of almost five hundred.

In addition to the educational advantages, the sisters worked to provide for the needs of the children and their families, principally through the generosity of the girls at Villa Maria and their parents. A clinic was established in 1962, named in honor of Sister M. Estella Rock, who had inspired the alumnae of Villa Marie to provide this much-needed health care for these children. A dental chair was donated by the Chilean Army in 1965 through the good services of General Carlos Hepp and Commander Xavier Palacios. Moreover, the Villa Marians contributed funds to purchase a truck which served the needs of the school and the campesinos as moving van, ambulance, and school bus!

The history of Escula San Francisco was marked by

anxious periods during the regime of the communist president, Salvador Allende, and in the period following his suicide, under the Junta Militar. However, the sisters were allowed to continue their work.

During the late seventies families began to move from Santiago out toward Las Condes and the land occupied by the campesinos rapidly escalated in value. The government moved several families from the poblaciones out to La Granga, an hour's distance away, which prevented the students' continued attendance at San Francisco. Eventually the Holy Cross Fathers decided that, if the poblaciones were moved, the school would not fulfill its original purpose of serving the poor and should be closed. Notified by government authorities of the precise date of eradication of the poblaciones, September 18, 1984,[57] Father Roberto Gilbo C.S.C. announced that the school would close at the termination of the current scholastic year.

It had already been decided by Mother Marie Genevieve, superior general, and the members of the council that despite decreasing membership in the congregation the sisters who had staffed San Francisco would continue to serve the underprivileged in Chile. Valle Hermosa, about fifty miles north of Santiago, in the diocese of San Felipe, was the site chosen for their future labors.[58] In March 1986 the sisters opened the covent Nuestro Senora del Rosario and began to teach religion in two public elementary schools and in one public high school. In addition, they organized classes for adult catechists.

The third foundation in Chile made by the congregation was that of San Mateo in Osorno. This city which toward the end of the sixties had a population of ninety thousand had been founded a century earlier by German immigrants who had been invited by the Chilean government to farm the land. In 1823, Chile had been the first country in the western hemisphere to abolish slavery. Over four hundred miles south of Santiago, Osorno is close to the southern extremity of the central valley with its fertile farmland.

The Jesuit rector of the San Mateo school had petitioned Mother Maria Pacis in 1967 to staff a school for young boys previously administered by a German congregation, the Fathers of the Divine Word.[59] Consequently, on March 18, 1968 the first faculty, consisting of Mother Charlotte Marie McCurdy, Sister Marian Pius Burns, Sister Maria Norma Comena, and Sister Estella Dolores Chappel, welcomed 306 boys in grades kindergarten through five. This proved to be a very difficult period in which to establish a school because of the unsettled economic conditions throughout the country, the frequent strikes, and the political unrest. The Jesuits enunciated the policy for San Mateo: "... following Christ's command that we love all men, San Mateo would not declare political allegiance to any party and would continue to serve all the people of Osorno regardless of their political affiliation."[60] The school increased in enrollment in spite of the problems mentioned above, and by 1974 reached 485. The majority of the students were from upper middle class families although the Jesuits had initiated an ambitious scholarship program to take care of the poor.

During 1974, a serious study of the situation was made by Mother Claudia and her council, because from the beginning it had been difficult to maintain a vibrant community life in Osorno. Pope Paul had declared: "... you nevertheless intend to create surroundings which are favorable to the spiritual progress of each member of the community.... There is no doubt that community spirit, relationships of friendship and fraternal cooperation in the same apostolate, as well as mutual support in a shared life chosen for a better service of Christ are so many valuable factors in this daily progress." [61]

It had become increasingly evident that three or four sisters living five hundred miles from the nearest I.H.M. convent could not be afforded the support and companionship necessary, so the decision was regretfully made to withdraw from this school as of January 1975.

The Jesuits of the Maryland Province continued to administer the school and to teach in the high school division, assisted by members of the laity. The institution has flourished, as is evidenced by the increase in enrollment, since a typical graduating class now numbers 125 in contrast to the 10 in the first year that the Jesuits staffed the school. There has been a reorganization and the school belongs to the Chilean province of Jesuits, although the Maryland province continues to assist in staffing it.[62]

Since the Alphonsian spirit of the congregation stresses service to the most abandoned, there had been a strong desire to open a mission in Peru for the evangelization and education of the very poor. San Antonio,[63] as noted above, had experienced great improvement in the economic conditions of the people in the surrounding area and the sisters wished to serve some children similar to those who had been taught in Callao in the twenties. A plea was received from Bishop Lorenzo Alvarado of Huacho, who declared that the sisters could do much for the people in the mountains who were in total spiritual abandonment.[64] In response, the first community consisting of Sister Maureen Margaret Illescas, Sister Edward Dolores Sullivan, and Sister Theresa Marian McCormick was appointed on July 16, 1972.[65]

At the present time, four sisters are carrying out very diversified operations in Barranca in their efforts to help these people grow in their knowledge and love of Christ.

In the local government schools they contact 1,760 girls for weekly instruction in religion.[66] Upon their arrival in Barranco the sisters had established a kindergarten with Sister Maureen Margaret, the superior of the convent San Ildephonso, as the teacher. In the intervening years, other grades were gradually added until the school, known as San Martin, currently has the full elementary program K–6, with an enrollment of 250 boys and girls. This parish school, under the direction of the pastor, Reverend Astocondor, has a program in which the sisters teach religion and lay faculty the other areas of the curriculum.

The training of catechists is an area to which the sisters devote much of their time and energy since this is the way they can vicariously reach the hundreds of persons whom the bishop had described as spiritually starved.[67] The importance of these catechists and the necessity of a thorough training for them was noted by the bishops in Vatican II: "Likewise worthy of praise are the ranks of men and women catechists, to whom missionary work among the nations owes so much. Animated with an apostolic spirit, they by their immense efforts make an outstanding and altogether necessary contribution to the spread of the faith and of the Church. . . . Therefore, their training must be so thorough and so well adapted to cultural advances . . . they can perform their tasks as superbly as can be."[68]

In the congregation, the tradition of preparing children and adults for the reception of the sacraments goes back to the earliest days in Monroe, Michigan. Like their predecessors of more than a century ago, the sisters in Barranca instruct groups of adults in sacramental preparation. Moreover, they work diligently planning the Eucharistic liturgy, and involving these adults in the planning so that they will not be present at this mystery of faith as strangers or silent spectators but "through a proper appreciation of the rites and prayers ... participate knowingly, devoutly and actively."[69]

Several passages in the documents of Vatican II call for a proper recognition of the dignity of every human person, based on the fact of his creation in the image of God. *Gaudium et Spes* declares: "Above all the education of youth from every social background has to be undertaken, so that there can be produced not only men and women of refined talents, but those great souled persons who are so desperately required by our times."[70] In the entire history of the Immaculate Heart education program the sisters in imitation of Saint Alphonsus have always welcomed students of every social background, and their undertakings in Latin America are no exception. Escuelita Gratuita Villa Maria was established in 1973 at La Planicie in one of the buildings of Villa Maria Academy, for the education of the sons and daughters of the poor workers in that suburb of Lima. Originally planned to consist only of the primaria, K–3, other levels were gradually added. At present, 227 students are enrolled in grades K–6.[71] All instruction is in Spanish but Sister Graciela, directora, has introduced a class in English for the more capable pupils. High standards of academic performance are maintained. The religious, moral, and aesthetic training which the sisters strive to impart to the students in their prestigious academy also characterizes the program of the escuelita.

An observer once commented that it was not an unusual sight to see a poor Indian woman, with an infant strapped to her back, guide her young son of kindergarten age through the gate at the same time that a high school girl from one of the wealthiest and most socially prominent families entered. He believed that the school was giving a concrete and most effective lesson which could be fruitful in years to come.[72]

As noted above, the scope of this present work does not permit detailed treatment of the work of the sisters in Latin America through the years, but it is hoped that in the future a complete history will be written. This brief sketch has been included here to verify the fact that the congregation is aware of the pressing need for evangelization and is zealously striving to respond to the call of Vatican II in this regard. The bishops pointed out that the present historical situation is leading humanity into a new stage and that the Church is summoned with special urgency to save and renew every creature. She wishes "to marshall the forces of all the faithful . . . [to] spread everywhere the Kingdom of Christ."[73]

Thus, through the apostolate of the Catholic schools, the sisters have labored both north and south of the equator to make Christ better known and loved. Borrowing from the message of Pope Paul VI to youth, each day every member of the congregation prays in the following words:

> O God, we are about to begin our day's work in school. Help us to receive our students in Your Name. Bound by charity to one another and to them may we be penetrated by an apostolic spirit and may we give witness to Christ, the unique Teacher, by our lives as well as by our teachings.
>
> With the aid of your Spirit, may we inspire our students to open their hearts to the dimensions of the world, to heed the appeal of their brothers, to place their youthful energies at their service and to build with joyful enthusiasm a better world.
>
> May our example call them to be generous, pure, respectful, and sincere and to find in Christ, the Prophet of truth and love, the Companion and Friend of youth. Amen.

One of the earliest traditions of the Sisters of I.H.M. is to spend time during the summer in catechetical activity. On July 27, 1848 the sisters at Monroe received the first group of "fourteen Irish and two Canadians."[74] They devoted their time and attention to instructing these girls and preparing them for reception of the sacraments of Penance, Holy Eucharist, and Confirmation. The record shows that Bishop LeFevre administered Confirmation at the end of October before they returned to their homes.

The Vatican II document on Renewal of Religious Life reminds religious that each institute's sound traditions should be faithfully accepted and retained for these constitute a portion of the patrimony of the institute.[75] This early tradition has endured through the years, although instead of bringing a small group of children to the convent, the present-day I.H.M.s go out to them.

During the summer months catechetical instruction for children and the training of adult catechists are tasks that occupy approximately two hundred sisters each year. Although programs are conducted where needed in parishes in which the sisters teach during the academic year, to provide for those students enrolled in public rather than parochial school, a great emphasis in the summer is on areas where students do not have access to a Catholic education during the regular session. In a typical season, the sisters travel[76] to New York, Pennsylvania, New Jersey, Virginia, North Carolina, Georgia, Texas, New Mexico, the jungles of Peru, and the least cultivated sections of Chile to bring the Word of God to the inhabitants, and in some areas to develop programs whereby others are prepared to continue catechetical instruction throughout the school year.

In this way they are responding to the call of the bishops enunciated in the fourth General Assembly of the

Synod in 1976. As Pope John Paul II stated, they stressed the urgency of giving catechesis definite priorities over other initiatives, less essential even if more spectacular, since the absolutely original aspect of the Church's mission is carried out by means of it. In his apostolic exhortation on this topic he gave this injunction: "Let the [religious] communities dedicate as much as possible of what ability and means they have to the specific work of catechesis."[77]

Programs are tailored to the specific needs of each center but the essence of all is the formal teaching of basic Christian doctrine, coupled with participation in meaningful liturgies and paraliturgical services. The objective is to make religion an important part of the daily lives of the children.

One such venture in Blackstone, Virginia was enthusiastically described in the local newspaper.[78] In this truly missionary territory there is only one priest within three hundred square miles and the assistance of the sisters has been deeply appreciated. With a bus provided by an urban parish in northern Virginia, the sisters started out each morning at 7:30a.m. to pick up the children in the various towns and along the countryside for the session which began at 9:00a.m. It was noted that while the program resembled Vacation Bible schools of other denominations, the Catholic one was not restricted to their own members but was open to everyone in the community. Instruction and activities lasted until noon when the sisters and their students set out on the return bus trip. This time was utilized in teaching and practicing hymns.

In the seventh year of its existence, the program which originally included approximately thirty-two students had grown to one hundred. The reporter characterized it as a "rare occurence—the work of six beautiful sisters; not family sisters, but rather sisters of love, sisters of God, Sisters of the Immaculate Heart of Mary, order of the Catholic church."

Immediately after the Council, the congregation responded to the appeal of the Archdiocese of Philadelphia and the Diocese of Arlington, Virginia, to supply sisters for full-time, year-long positions in the diocesan offices of religious education. Especially in Philadelphia, an intensive summer program was developed[79] to provide catechetical instruction, in an effort to reach the Catholic students enrolled in public schools.[80] Sister Maria Cabrini Bompadre, I.H.M., and later Sister Marita Joan O'Donnell, I.H.M., served as supervisor of the C.C.D summer vacation program in which more than one hundred sisters taught. In addition, a sister was assigned full time in the office of the Spanish apostolate in both the Archdiocese of Philadelphia and the diocese of Allentown to ensure that the growing number of Hispanics would receive catechetical instruction. For the Spanish population in Philadelphia, West Chester, Reading, Kennett Square, and Easton catechetical programs were also planned and staffed by the sisters.[81] For the visually impaired, religious instruction was provided in Saint Lucy School until the children were capable of being mainstreamed into the classes at Saint Francis de Sales School, both staffed by the congregation.[82]

In order to update and perfect their methods in catechetics, twenty-two sisters have enrolled in the Notre Dame Pontifical Catechetical Institute originally based in Middleburg, Virginia but presently in Arlington, Virginia, receiving degrees from the Angelicum in Rome and certificates from the Sacred Congregation of the Clergy in Rome. These sisters, after completing their studies, offered workshops and courses to the postulants and novices, as well as to sisters in the active apostolate thus providing many with a solid basis and up-to-date techniques for the instruction they later imparted to hundreds of students. One of the earliest graduates of the Institute, Sister Saint Mark, currently serves as assistant dean of the program.[83]

In their efforts at evangelization the sisters have been mindful of the words of Pope John Paul II: "For 'renewal of spirit' will be authentic and will have real fruitfulness in the Church, not so much as it gives rise to extraordinary charisms, but according as it leads the greatest possible number of the faithful, as they travel their daily paths, to make a humble, and patient, persevering effort to know the mystery of Christ better and to bear witness to it."[84]

CHAPTER IV

Formation for Witness: Professional Preparation

Several statements in Vatican II documents noted the concern of the Council Fathers that religious be educated "... in doctrine and technical matters, even to the extent of winning appropriate degrees" and that "as far as possible, superiors should provide them with the opportunity, resources and time to do so."[1]

Throughout the years the congregation had striven for excellence in the education of the sisters for their work in the apostolate. Before the establishment of Immaculata College, the institution which eventually conferred degrees on the great majority of the sisters, professors from the University of Pennsylvania and from West Chester State University conducted courses at Villa Maria, West Chester.[2] A new venture in advanced education was inaugurated in 1917, when application was made to Reverend Hugh A. Gallagher, O.S.A., at Villanova for faculty members to give extension classes for the sisters at Immaculata.[3] With the authorization of Reverend Edward G. Dohan, O.S.A., president of Villanova, courses commenced February 11, 1917, at Immaculata with the president and Rev. Joseph A. Hickey, O.S.A., as professors and during the ensuing summer the first Villanova Summer School was conducted at Immaculata. In 1918,[4] at the request of other religious communities, the summer program was transferred to the Villanova campus, and in 1931 an additional center was established at Hallahan High School in Philadelphia. Saturday sessions were introduced in the fall of 1918 on the Villanova Campus and in 1931 at the Hallahan center. In 1928, evening courses were offered at Villanova but after six years it was found that a greater number could be served at the Hallahan extension.

When the Commonwealth of Pennsylvania granted the charter to Immaculata College on November 12, 1920,[5] it became possible to provide summer sessions on campus for sisters to pursue courses leading to the baccalaureate degree and to teacher certification, and by August 1985, 2,085 sisters had been awarded degrees. (*See* appendix B for statistics.)

To supply the need for graduate education, sisters had also been assigned to Catholic University and the University of Pennsylvania, receiving degrees as early as 1914. As many sisters as possible during the ensuing years pursued graduate study, in a slow but steady growth, so that the superiors of the congregation felt that they had been in line with the mind of the Church when Pope Pius XII, in September 1951, addressed the First International Congress of Teaching Sisters with these words: "This presupposes that your teaching Sisters are masters of the subjects they expound. See to it, therefore, that they are well trained, and that their education corresponds in quality and academic degrees to that demanded by the state."[6]

In the sixties and seventies the number of those attaining advanced degrees (*See* appendix C) increased significantly for several reasons. The total membership of the congregation had increased greatly in the decade of the sixties as well as the number who had completed baccalaureate programs. Moreover, candidates entering the congregation tended to have completed more work on the collegiate level than had been true in the past. On the national scene, the post-Sputnik emphasis on science and mathematics led to many opportunities for scholarships and fellowships, so that many sisters received grants for advanced study.

In the years 1968–81 grants were awarded to 336 sisters, and consequently, sisters of the congregation were present on 152 campuses in 35 states and 9 foreign countries. The variety of institutions attended,[7] with the wide geographic spread undoubtedly enriched not only the sisters who attended but, through subsequent sharing, the faculty and students in their respective schools.

Since 1969, nineteen sisters attained the doctoral degree. They attended the following universities: University of Pennsylvania, University of Pittsburgh, University of Rochester, Catholic University of America, St. Louis University, Bryn Mawr College, University of Virginia, Temple University, Case Western Reserve University, Fordham University, University of Missouri, University of Wisconsin, Rutgers University, and the Angelicum in Rome. During this period three sisters were also awarded honorary degrees.

The Bishops of the United States in their pastoral letter *To Teach as Jesus Did* declared: "In the Catholic school instruction in religious truth and values is an integral part of the school program. It is not one more subject alongside the rest, but it is perceived and functions as the underlying reality in which the student's experiences of learning and living achieve their coherence and deepest meaning."[8]

Therefore priorities for the training of sisters were

established with religious studies as the highest. Since Vatican II brought in its wake intensified interest in Sacred Scripture and theology, there was perceived a need to update all members of the congregation in these areas. More sisters were engaged in programs leading to baccalaureate degrees with concentration in theology and in M.A. programs in theology than in any other field, e.g. 364 completed in 1968–74 and 286 in 1975–81. Every year during this period at least one, and more often two, sisters were released for full-time study in theology during the school year.[9]

A significant contribution was made by the congregation in regard to the program in religious studies established at Saint Charles Seminary[10] in Philadelphia. In 1968, Sister Mary Hubert Curran, who as a member of the general council was charged with the education of the sisters, had spoken with several members of the clergy about the feasibility of courses in theology being offered in a summer session at Saint Charles Seminary. Apparently, authorities in other congregations engaged in education had also voiced this same interest, and as a result Cardinal Krol issued an invitation to the principal communities to meet with him. Cardinal Krol and Monsignor Thomas Welsh, rector of Saint Charles (later Bishop), met at the seminary with representatives of the communities to discuss a program which was implemented in 1969. This satisfied the need for a theology program of high scholarly level with sound doctrinal content. Eventually couses were also offered in an evening session during the scholastic year and the program was expanded, leading not only to the degree master of arts in religious studies, but also to a diploma from the Sacred Congregation for the Clergy, Rome.[11] Later expansions included the introduction of a program on ministerial music in cooperation with the Archdiocesan Music Office.

This program planned in collaboration with the Commission on Sacred Music is designed to implement the directive of the Constitution on Sacred Liturgy,[12] that training centers for church musicians be established to provide practical training in various skills for parish musicians.

Since its inception, the Sisters, Servants of the Immaculate Heart of Mary have strongly supported the program. The first degree awarded, in the division of religious studies, August 1973, was to Sister Edward Marie Dougherty, I.H.M., and in subsequent years, 101 of the total 432 degrees granted were earned by Sisters, Servants of the Immaculate Heart of Mary.[13] More than three hundred additional sisters have participated in courses for enrichment or as candidates for certificates. Sister Cor Immaculatum, I.H.M., has served as assistant academic dean of the division since 1974.[14] Sister Eileen Dolores, I.H.M., professor of psychology at Immaculata College, has frequently served as a visiting professor at the seminary. Several other sisters have given occasional courses.

Two other opportunities were made available to the sisters to update their knowledge of theology. A forum on contemporary moral problems[15] was held at Immaculata College with Monsignor Francis X. DeLorenzo (currently rector of Saint Charles Seminary) as lecturer. The program consisted of one meeting weekly for five weeks and a lecture followed by a question period. Approximatley three hundred sisters participated.

Three-week institutes which consisted of courses in liturgy, Sacred Scripture, and *The Church in the Modern World* were offered at Lynchburg, Virginia and Villa Maria House of Studies during the summers of 1969–74 and a total of 649 sisters took advantage of this opportunity. Visiting professors from three religious congregations—Redemptorists, Holy Ghost Fathers and Passionists—conducted these classes.[16] The document on Catholic Education[17] entreats teachers to: "carry on magnanimously in their chosen task, and to strive to excel in penetrating their students with the spirit of Christ, in the art of teaching, and in the advancement of knowledge. Thus they will not only foster the internal renewal of the Church, but will safeguard and intensify her beneficial presence in the world of today, especially in the world of the intellect."

Since approximately 75 percent of the sisters in the active apostolate were engaged in the elementary schools, a decision of the 1969 chapter[18] was that high priority be given to training sisters in the area of elementary education, and this was implemented in several ways. In the ensuing six years 352 sisters completed programs leading to degrees and certification in elementary education, including two on the doctoral level. The total enrollment of sisters in courses concerned specifically with methodology on the elementary level reached the 2,225 mark during this period. A special effort was made to have sisters teaching on the seventh and eighth grade level apply for grants for which they were academically qualified. The eighty-two sisters who attained such grants principally in the areas of mathematics, science, geography, and social studies attended forty-three institutions located in eighteen states.[19] The special segment of early childhood education was emphasized on the collegiate level when Immaculata College attained recognition from the Pennsylvania Department of Education for its program in early childhood education.[20] Moreover, two sisters were released from the active apostolate to study abroad for a year, examining the educational systems of Great Britain, especially the British Infant Schools, and the Open Schools.[21] The methods of Dr. Maria Montessori were examined by two sisters who attained certification as Montessori teachers.

Under the benefits of Pennsylvania Act 194,[22] funds were available for special courses to be offered at Immaculata College in the techniques of teaching and 551 sisters profited by enrolling in these.

In 1970, on the occasion of the golden jubilee of the college, a proposal was made by a trustee that the board of trustees consider the advisability of initiating a graduate program in elementary education, since there was no institution between West Chester and Philadelphia which granted an advanced degree in that area, although at that particular time there was a great demand for such degrees. For example, at West Chester State approximately six applicants were competing for each place. Moreover, no Catholic institution in the Philadelphia area granted this degree, and it seemed eminently fitting that Catholic philosophy enliven the curriculum in this crucial field of the education of our youth. Because there were several large communities of teaching religious in the vicinity of Philadelphia this was deemed a means of service to the Church.[23] However, the board considered it wise to defer the introduction of a new program in view of a scheduled evaluation by the Middle States Association of Colleges and Secondary Schools in 1974, so the graduate program was not introduced until 1983, with a three-pronged curriculum including counseling, psychology, and nutrition education as well as educational leadership and administration.[24]

By these efforts to provide sound professional preparation, the congregation endeavored to foster the corporate commitments made in the past. Indeed, it had been called to do so by these words of Pope John Paul II:

> The ecclesial dimension of your vocation ... means that institutes are called to continue to foster, in dynamic faithfulness, those corporate commitments

which were related to the original charism, which were authenticated by the Church, and which still fulfill important needs of the people of God. A good example in this regard would be the Catholic School system which has been invaluable for the Church in the United States, an excellent means not only for communicating the Gospel of Christ to the students, but also for permeating the entire community with Christ's truth and His love. It is one of the apostolates in which women religious have made and are still making, an incomparable contribution.[25]

The congregation provided the opportunity for sisters to fulfil the academic requirements for teacher certification in the various states in which their schools are located. In Pennsylvania, as early as the twenties, sisters qualified for provisional certification but permanent certificates for sisters were valid only in nonpublic schools, since at that time one condition for attaining permanent certification was teaching three years in a public school of the commonwealth. It was not until 1970 that the statute was amended by the deletion of the word *public*, since it was pointed out that by that time Act 194 conferred benefits on teachers in nonpublic schools, provided they held permanent certification—an obvious contradiction.[26]

Because the Council Fathers had reiterated the importance of the education of teachers, declaring that they "should be trained with particular care so that they may be enriched with both secular and religious knowledge, appropriately certified, and may be equipped with an educational skill that reflects modern day findings,"[27] the congregation intensified its efforts to seek proper teacher certification for the members, and since 1969 the total number of certificates attained has passed the seventeen hundred mark.

The congregation performed a service for religious and secular teachers in parochial schools by contesting a practice of the Department of Teacher Certification in Pennsylvania which refused to recognize credits in theology earned by students who were seeking to attain the twenty-four semester hours of postbaccalaureate work required to convert a provisional certificate to a permanent one. In February 1981 the matter eventually reached the chief state counsel, Michael A. Davis, who decided in favor of the position of the Sisters, Servants of the Immaculate Heart of Mary and thus ensured that such courses could be validly included in the required twenty-four semester hours. This was particularly beneficial to lay teachers who were graduates of nonsectarian institutions and were seeking to complete eighteen semester hours in theology required by the Archdiocese of Philadelphia as well as twenty-four semester hours of postbaccalaureate work required for Pennsylvania certification. (*See* appendix E.)

In the period 1964–84 many innovations and advances in educational technology had brought about noticeable changes in pedagogical methods across the country. To enable the sisters to keep abreast of these, workshops on the elementary level and in the various disciplines on the secondary level were offered. For example, courses in the use of the computer were made available as soon as it became evident that it would play a significant role in future educational programs. A sister was assigned to prepare for a Ph.D. in mathematics in the area of computer science, and became the first recipient of that degree at the University of Illinois at Urbana.[28] She later participated as a faculty member in many courses in computer assisted instruction set up throughout the country by the National Science Foundation for teachers in secondary schools. The record shows that workshops under community auspices were organized in all the following areas: art, biology, chemistry, elementary science, foreign languages, geography, home economics, language arts, linguistics, mathematics, music, religion, and social studies. These were staffed by visiting professors, Immaculata faculty, consultants from diocesan education offices, public schools, and industry. The total registration annually reached two thousand. On the elementary level, "sharing days " provided both demonstration of techniques and displays of materials utilized, as well as projects executed by pupils.

The document *Ad Gentes* showed the concern of the Council Fathers for the education of students who, because they were born in developing nations, had special needs: "With special care let them devote themselves to the education of children and young people by means of different kinds of schools. These schools should be considered not only as an outstanding means for forming and developing Christian youth, but also as a service of supreme value to men, especially in developing nations, a service elevating the level of human dignity, and preparing the way for living conditions which are more human."[29]

The flourishing apostolate in Peru and Chile has been described above,[30] and has been the object of attention during the past sixty years. Within the past twenty-five years the sizable influx of Puerto Ricans and Cubans into the parishes in the United States in which our sisters serve made it imperative for even greater numbers of sisters to acquire fluency in the Spanish language. Sisters were enrolled in courses in Spanish and Latin American studies in the Catholic University of Chile, Catholic University of Puerto Rico, the Pontifical Catholic University of Peru, University of Madrid, University of Mexico, University of Wisconsin, University of Pittsburgh, Case Western Reserve University, Georgetown University, Millersville College,

Villanova University, as well as Immaculata College. In 1976, a Spanish house was established at Immaculata during the summer session which provided the experience of total immersion in the language for the participants.[31] The community collaborated with the archdiocese of Philadelphia in offering Programmatic Spanish, the Foreign Service Institute plan for learning to communicate in this language. This was administered by Sister Peter Mary, I.H.M., and several of the sisters took advantage of the sessions conducted both in the summer and during the scholastic year.[32]

Immaculata College, especially through the work of the Center for the Americas (1967), has been a valuable resource for all educators in the Philadelphia area who are concerned with the welfare of the Hispanics residing there. It has provided timely lectures on the political, social, and economic aspects of the various countries of Latin America, together with the opportunity of dialoguing with native scholars and diplomats who participate in these programs. A newsletter, *Puerto Ricans: Bridging the Gap,* issued by the center, is also productive and insightful.[33] The congregation has also cooperated by supplying a sister as professor of Spanish for Villanova University in Madrid,[34] and at Saint Charles Seminary in Overbrook, so that seminarians might be trained for apostolic service in parishes with large Hispanic populations.[35]

The most significant accomplishment in this area was the establishment of a master's degree program in bicultural/bilingual studies at Immaculata College. Teachers, social workers, counselors, and administrators in the area of West Chester experienced the need for a bilingual/bicultural program in order to gain the competency required to serve the Hispanics who were settling there in increasing numbers. The director of bilingual education in West Chester requested Immaculata to inaugurate a graduate bicultural/bilingual studies program to meet the desperate need for teachers of children with limited English proficiency.

Since at that time Immaculata College offered only undergraduate courses, the I.H.M. Sisters in Scranton agreed to cooperate in establishing a program in which all courses are offered at Immaculata and the degree awarded by Marywood. Since its inception in 1977, thirty-six degrees have been awarded both to Sisters of I.H.M. and to other educators, many of whom have been assisted by scholarships, since the program has received federal grants each year.[36]

The founder of the Center for the Americas and the prime mover in the establishment of the degree program, Sister Mary Consuela Callaghan, has been honored by many national organizations for her outstanding contribution to the Hispanics. During the annual conference of the National Association for Bilingual Education in 1986 the program at Immaculata College was selected as one of six outstanding programs in the United States.

Just as the congregation had collaborated with Saint Charles Seminary in the establishment of the master's program in religious studies, a very profitable program leading to M.Ed. with specialization in reading was inaugurated in cooperation with the Virginia Polytechnic Institute.[37] The college agreed to send professors from Blacksburg, Virginia, to a site in northern Virginia to conduct the couses in a core curriculum, with students spending one summer on campus to fulfill requirements in electives. The great advantage of the arrangement was that sisters could reside in convents, avoid spending time traveling, and utilize the Library of Congress and other facilities in the Washington area. In the first cycle of the program the Sisters of Notre Dame of Chardon, Ohio participated to make up the full complement of twenty-eight students; in the second five years it was an exclusively I.H.M. program, based at Saint James in Falls Church. All the participants, both faculty and students enthusiastically endorsed the program.

The Council Fathers had considered the appropriate education of religious during their deliberations and summarized their conclusions as follows: "In suitable residences and in a fitting manner let them [religious] continue their training in the religious life and the apostolate, in doctrine and technical matters, even to the extent of winning appropriate degrees. . . . As far as possible, superiors should provide them with the opportunity, the resources, and the time to do so."[38]

There is substantial evidence that such opportunity, resources and time have been provided to the Sisters, Servants of the Immaculate Heart of Mary throughout these years.

The documents of Vatican II remind teachers that it depends chiefly on them whether the Catholic school achieves its purpose.[39] Therefore, teachers "should be prepared for their work with special care, having the appropriate qualifications and adequate learning, both religious and secular. They should also be skilled in the art of education in accordance with the discoveries of modern times."

In addition to qualified teachers, in order to reach high levels of excellence, schools must have inspiring leadership and good instructional materials. The Sisters, Servants of the Immaculate Heart have considered it urgent to supply these needs.

During the years sisters have served in important posts in the education departments of the Archdiocese of Philadelphia and the Dioceses of Allentown, Arlington, Harrisburg, and Richmond. The wise planning and projections of the Superintendents of Schools and their associates in these offices have guided and stabilized the schools in these times of difficulty and uncertainty. Many sisters have also served on the various curriculum committees in the dioceses in which the congregation serves.

In the area of administration, Sister Carmel Regina Shields completed an in-depth study of supervision and devised a supervision approach especially appropriate for the Catholic elementary school. In collaboration with Dr. Allan Glatthorn of the University of Pennsylvania she authored a useful volume, *Differentiated Supervision for Catholic Elementary Schools*.[40]

In regard to appropriate instructional materials, the sisters have made an outstanding contribution in the production of two widely acclaimed series of textbooks for the elementary schools, *Voyages in English* and *Progress in Arithmetic*. The former series, begun in 1939 by Sister M. Donatus McNickle, was brought to completion by Sister Francis Borgia Connors and Sister Rose Anita McDonnell, assisted by sisters who were specialists on each of the grade levels. Now in its second revision, this text has been used by over a million pupils in every state in the nation, as well as Puerto Rico and the Philippines. Both revisions were undertaken by Sister Francis Borgia assisted by a committee of sisters, and the most recent one was completed shortly before her death in 1985. A new edition is in preparation under the direction of Sister Carolyn Marie Dimick.

During the decade of the sixties, another English series was launched—*Power Tools in English*. Sister Saint Ignatius Martin assisted by a committee of sisters prepared these texts in which the principal emphasis was on creative writing. This provided a useful supplement to *Voyages in English*.

Sister Rose Anita, along with Sister Francis Borgia, has received both national and international recognition for her contribution in the field of education. In the significant changes which took place in the method of presenting mathematical concepts during the late fifties and early sixties, a committee of sisters, chaired by Sister Maria Socorro Picirillo, had studied the new trends as early as 1961. Their objective was to keep abreast of the develoments in this discipline and to assess their effect upon the parochial school program and course of study. Their study eventuated in preliminary outline of the scope to be assigned to each grade level, and in the launching of a new textbook series, *Improving Computational Skills*. Between 1963 and 1966, books one through six were prepared by Sister Rose Anita and Sister Mary Clarence Kilgariff, assisted by a group of sisters. Books seven and eight were prepared by Reverend Stanley Bezuska, S.J., assisted, likewise, by a committee of I.H.M. sisters. A new series *New Progress in Mathematics*, was completed in 1985 by Sister Rose Anita, assisted by a committee of I.H.M. Sisters. It has met with an enthusiastic reception and has been placed on the approved lists of many public school systems, including those of Philadelphia and New York. It has contributed to the training of hundreds of thousands of students.

Another text was prepared by Sister Joseph Kieran McAdams for advanced students. Sister had assisted Dr. B.E. Gillett in the preparation of his work *Introduction to Operations Research: A Computer-Oriented Algorithmic Apprach*. She is coauthor of *Text and Manual*.

A more recent publication on a much smaller scale, *Catholics and American History*, is the work of Sister Edward William Quinn and Sister Margaret Rose Adams. Released in September, 1985, this black line master book provides a supplement to the American history series published by Allyn and Bacon, supplying teachers on the fifth grade level with material regarding the Catholic contribution to the history of our country.

In a much publicized report of Dr. Paul Vitz, professor

of psychology at New York University, there is convincing evidence that the social studies textbooks currently used in United States schools show "total absence of any primary religious text about typical contemporary American religious life." This study, conducted under the auspices of the United States Department of Education, was based on an analysis of sixty textbooks most widely used across the nation. The ten sets of texts examined are used by an estimated 87 percent of the nation's elementary school pupils. Commenting on the report one journalist stated, "Religion, it appears, is something that happened long ago and far away."[41] Since the Department of Education authorized the study, it is possible that steps will be taken in the future to fill these lacunae. In producing this small supplement it may be that I.H.M.s were on the cutting edge of an eduational development.

In summary, during this period since 1962 the congregation has continued its tradition of seeking excellence in the Catholic school. As the document *Catholic Schools* states, "Catholic schools are receiving more and more attention since the Second Vatican Council, especially with the emphasis now being placed on the church as portrayed in the constitutions, *Lumen Gentium* and *Gaudium et Spes*. . . . [The Church] considers them as a privileged means of promoting the formation of the whole man, since the school is a center in which a specific concept of the world, of man, and of history is developed and conveyed."[42]

CHAPTER V

Exchange of Witness: Community Life and Spirit

The bishops assembled in Vatican II stressed that common life, fashioned on the model of the early Church where the body of believers were united in heart and soul, "should continue to be lived in prayer and the communion of the same spirit."[1] Believing that unity is not only a "visible pledge that Christ will return (Jn 13:35; 17:21) and a source of great apostolic energy,"[2] the members of the chapter who drew up the revised constitutions of the Sisters, Servants of the Immaculate Heart of Mary were convinced that each sister had a right to the spiritual strength and moral support of every other sister. Therefore, the constitutions provided that as a local community the sisters, recognizing the Eucharist as the center and animating force in their lives, participate together in the Eucharistic liturgy each day.[3] Pope John Paul II had reiterated the importance of the Eucharist[4] when addressing religious in Siena as follows: "Therefore it is necessary to see to it that the Eucharistic mystery . . . always has in each of our communities . . . that central position which fully and rightly belongs to it . . . the Council reminds us (LG7) as we actually partake of the body of the Lord, we are elevated to communion *with Him* (personal relationship) and *among ourselves* (communitarian relationship)."

Moreover, in accordance with the mandate of Vatican II,[5] to adapt the manner of praying to modern physical and psychological circumstances of the members and the demands of the apostolate, the recitation of Lauds and Vespers of the Divine Office was adopted in order to participate more intimately in the liturgical life of the Church. Provision was also made to give a larger space to mental prayer rather than to a multitude of prayers. The pious exercises commonly accepted in the Church, i.e., the Rosary and Way of the Cross,[6] were retained since these are an integral part of Alphonsian spirituality.

In their efforts to deepen the spirit of prayer in the congregation, the sisters were responding to Pope Paul's admonition, "Be souls of prayer . . . it is part of your vocation to confront a society which puts value only on visible results."[7] In the midst of a very active life they strove to be mindful of his assurance that "a period of real oration has more value than the greatest activity, even it it be apostolic."

Two forces present in the schools of the sixties had an impact on the community life of the sisters; first, the declining number of sisters assigned to each school, and second, the increasing number of lay teachers. As Pope John Paul II stressed the importance of community life, which has been a characteristic of religious through the ages and which is a necessary element in creating, developing, and perpetuating spiritual bonds, he called upon major superiors to "make every effort that this community life may be facilitated and loved, becoming in this way a precious means of mutual help and personal fulfillment."[8]

The major superiors of the I.H.M.s sought to carry out his injunction by combining faculties of schools which were conveniently located for such combinations. Each case was examined individually and given careful consideration in conformity with the injunction in *Ecclesiae Sanctae:* "Religious superiors who, for whatever reason ask for the suppression of any house or work, should not do so hastily."[9]

In the period between 1977 and 1985, seventeen[10] such mergers resulted in local communities numerous enough to foster genuine exchange and mutual support. Moreover, the problem of maintaining a fairly large convent for comparatively few sisters was eliminated; the energy of the sisters could then be channelled to other areas. An additional economic benefit accrued to the pastors who then shared the expense of a single facility.

In at least one instance—Immaculate Heart, Chester—this financial saving was a significant factor in keeping the school open, as the pastor had appealed to the community to take the step of closing the convent because of his great economic difficulties. One of the earliest foundations in Pennsylvania, Immaculate Heart, Chester, had been established in 1883. Over the more recent years of its history, as the neighborhood changed from one in which the parishioners were predominantly Irish to the present black population, the sisters had labored to create a loving faith community in which non-Catholic children felt truly welcome in the school. This inner-city school had been able to accomplish much not only for its students but also the whole community area; therefore, every effort was made to assure its survival. In 1973, the school had been the recipient of a federal government grant under title III for a program, "Individulization—Gateway to Self-direction." Some excerpts from the reports of the government evaluators give a pen picture of the school's atmosphere.

12/4/73
Dr. Zelechoski
Forest City Regional School District
Forest City, Pa. 18421

... The Immaculate Heart of Mary School has something *special*. I'm, sure it's not only the Title II Program which I found to be a noble educational endeavor. I'm sure it's not only a dedicated principal and staff. The hardworking aides are not the entire secret. The eager, mindful, well-disciplined youngsters were a joy to observe. Your school is clean, but that is not your secret.

Under the direction of Sister Joseph Anthony, from parents to students, all who work within its walls, the I.H.M. School is Hope. You have Faith. I felt the Charity of I.H.M. when I was in the presence of its people.

I have found your secret. It is your Faith, Hope, and Love.

Evaluation 10/15/74

Mr. Oliver Alexander
Principal
Ridley Park Junior High School

There are few opportunities to experience genuine feelings of love in what could be a hostile atmosphere. Schools can be a battleground. What is voiced administratively as sound educationally is often inhuman and impersonal.

The experience at I.H.M. was unique, for it portrayed black and white working together under the Lord's grand design of all people helping one another. It is our desire that the projects undertaken in the name of individualization flourish, for the work here is important. Important for the people here, yes, but also as a symbol to all people of what can happen when people dedicate themselves to a noble cause—the education of the youth of this great country.

> Dr. Ross L. Burtner
> Ass. Supt. of Instruction
> Title III Evaluator
> Coatesville Area School District
>
> I was greatly impressed by the creative manner in which an old school has been renovated within, through the intelligent use of color, lighting, walls, and carpeting. An abundance of fresh-looking instructional materials was also in evidence. But most of all I was impressed with the loving concern and positive attitudes shown toward the children by teachers, aides, foster grandparents—and the involvement of the community in the school. The principal deserves high praise for a leadership role in providing an excellent model of humane, Christian education in the heart of an inner city that needs a lot of loving concern.

In view of the urgent need to maintain this Catholic school it was deemed advisable to accede to the request of the pastor and alleviate the financial difficulty of maintaining a convent, since the sisters could join the community of Saint Madeline convent in nearby Ridley Park. As in the case of the other decisions to combine faculties of two or more schools in one convent the congregation was demonstrating its awareness of the guidelines laid down in *Lumen Gentium*: "Religious families give to their members the support of greater stability in their way of life; a proven method of acquiring perfection; fraternal association."[11]

By means of the procedure of joining two faculties in one convent, the community offered sisters an atmosphere in which they could evidence the authenticity of their witness and contribute to greater apostolic efficacy. The sisters were called both to enjoy the fruits of community life and to confront its challenges. Pope John Paul II beautifully describes this life:

> Living in a religious community is a concrete expression of love for others and the secret of a serene and harmonious personal maturation. Acceptance of one's brother with his qualities and his limitations, the effort to coordinate one's own initiatives with decisions matured together, the self-criticism imposed by continuous confrontation with the evaluations and view points of others, become not only a very effective training ground of human and Christian virtues but also a precious opportunity for constant verification of the earnestness with which one endeavors to put into practice in one's life the obligations assumed in the religious profession.[12]

In the area of common life it is appropriate to mention the wearing of the religious habit, which according to Vatican II should be "simple and modest, poor and at the same time becoming . . . it must meet the requirements of health and be suited to the circumstances of time and place and to the needs of the ministry involved."[13] The bishops then laid on religious the injunction to change any habit not in conformity with these norms. As a result, by January 1970, the habit of the Sisters of I.H.M. was shortened, the headpiece modified, and the fifteen-decade rosary replaced by a five-decade one, thus eliminating features that had caused accidents in former times. After further study, in 1982, a lighter weight habit, of a lighter shade of blue, was introduced for summer wear and for year-round wear in Southern localities. Through these adjustments the stipulations of *Perfectae Caritatis* have been met, and the sisters have retained, as Pope Paul VI urged, a dress that is "a sign of consecration . . . and in some way different from forms that are clearly secular."[14] Moreover, by continuing to wear a habit, the sisters comply with the many requests made by Pope John Paul II, who in the spirit of the teachings of Vatican II, declared it a measure of the deep reality of consecration to God,[15] and asked priests and religious not to "help the trend toward taking God off the street by adopting secular modes of dress and behavior. . . ."[16]

An important aspect of common life is the exercise of the virtue of poverty according to the manner vowed in each congregation. The Sisters, Servants of the Immaculate Heart of Mary, in the Alphonsian spirit of humility and simplicity, recognize their condition as needy and helpless before God, renounce the right to use and dispose of temporal goods without the permission of the superior, and embrace the condition in which the congregation furnishes them with their personal needs, in a manner consistent with the common life and the witness of poverty.

In conformity with the rule, the members exercise a corporate apostolate in education; contracts are entered into by the congregation, not the individual members; and the recompense involved is directed to the congregation.

Pope Paul VI reminded religious that they must not be afraid to say that religious life is difficult, for the struggle Saint Paul attributes to every Christian (1Cor. 9: 24–27) is revealed more explicitly in the life lived according to the evangelical counsels.[17] Moreover, in another context he pointed out that Vatican Council II stressed that the necessary submission to the law of labor, earning a living, and assisting the poor by their work are duties incumbent on religious.[18]

A decision of the Supreme Court in 1971 resulted in the cutting off of state aid to nonpublic schools and left many of the schools in which the sisters taught in very precarious condition. To help alleviate this burden, Mother Claudia, superior general of the Sisters, Servants of the Immaculate Heart of Mary and Mother Alice Anita, superior general of the Sisters of Saint Joseph in Philadelphia agreed as a witness to the importance of the Catholic school and as a sacrifice in the practice of poverty to forego the increase in salary projected for the ensuing year. They addressed[19] Cardinal Krol as follows:

> Your Eminence:
> In response to the financial crisis which now faces the Archdiocese of Philadelphia as a result of the Supreme Court decision curtailing aid to nonpublic schools, the Sisters, Servants of the Immaculate Heart of Mary and the Sisters of Saint Joseph, in consultation with their general councils, have agreed to sacrifice for the scholastic year of 1971–72 the increase in salary granted recently to their teaching religious.
>
> In public witness to their enduring dedication to Catholic education this sacrifice, in view of rising costs of living, professional education, and care of the sick and aged, will testify to their willingness as persons bound by the vow of poverty to be, as the Church asks, poor in fact, as well as in spirit.
>
> This is in keeping with the original spirit of their founders whose dedication to their apostolate flowed from the total gift of self expressed in their consecrated life according to the evangelical counsels of poverty, chastity, and obedience.

In his response, the cardinal acknowledged that the offer was most tempting since it entailed a gift of approximately $422,000, but he pointed out that the proposed increase in the salary of the sisters was barely adequate just to meet inflationary increases, and that the proposal imposes even greater austerity and sacrifices on the communities. Moreover, he pointed out that the deficit of 8.9 million dollars resulting from the cutting off of state aid made it incumbent on every sector of the total community to recognize responsibility to the children and to find new ways, new approaches, to financing the schools.[20]

The Sisters of I.H.M. made a similar offer to the bishops of the other dioceses in which they serve. Several of the bishops, as they gratefully accepted the offer, were lavish in their praise. One comment came from the auxiliary bishop of Belém, Pará, Brazil,[21] a country in which the congregation does not even serve. He wrote:

> Most Reverend Jude Prost, O.F.M.
> Belém, Pará, Brazil
> 10/2/71
>
> I am a stranger, yet after reading an article in the papers about your sisters I felt obliged to write. . . .
> God love and bless you, Mother, and all your sisters who offered to sacrifice a raise in salary in order to help keep our Catholic schools open. It is so good to hear of those noble acts of your sisters, acts that edify in these days and prove to the world that our sisters have not forgotten their mission in the world today.

Community Spirit

One very significant principle laid down by the bishops of Vatican II is: "It serves the best interests of the Church for communities to have their own special character and purpose. Therefore, loyal recognition and safekeeping should be accorded to the spirit of founders, as also to all the particular goals and wholesome traditions which constitute the heritage of each community."[22] In discussing the universal call to holiness, they further pointed out that the holiness of the Church must be manifested in the fruits of grace which the Spirit produces in the lives of the faithful,[23] and they exhorted religious to be always mindful of the fact that daily through them the Church presents Christ both to believers and to nonbelievers.[24]

Father Gillet did not hesitate to say that the zeal with which a congregation devotes itself to the personal holiness of its members determines the strength or weakness of community spirit.[25] In a treatise on this topic, drawing a parallel to the parable of the wise and foolish virgins, he declared that the former store up the oil of kindliness and love, of tenderness, sympathy, and gentleness, of understanding, tolerance, and forgiveness.[26] Love of God and love of neighbor were his recurrent themes as he strove to inculcate a spirit of sacrifice enlivened by joy.

Sister M. Celestine, one of the three original sisters, recorded in her dairy: "The sacred memory of those early days has never faded away. The home was filled with light and life and love...."[27]

Community spirit, because it consists of intangibles and is the very warp and woof of community life, is sometimes perceived more clearly by those outside the congregation than within it, as the following pages indicate.

In 1976, when the Eucharistic Congress convened in Philadelphia, more than 1,500 I.H.M.s participated in the various liturgies, processions, and other activities, and more than 750 sisters served both before and during the Congress in various capacities. In preparation for the Congress, Mother M. Claudia requested the privilege of exposition of the Blessed Sacrament for perpetual adoration during the five weeks of the spiritual institute in which approximately 250 sisters participated. In granting the permission Cardinal Krol stated: "I am aware of the Immaculate Heart Community's devotion to the Blessed Sacrament. I am also aware that your own prayerful life in this regard is a significant example. The power of this love expressed in prayerful adoration during these requested days and nights of exposition will be the source of immeasurable blessings upon the Eucharistic Congress."[28]

Along with these "Marys" who were lending spiritual support, hundreds of I.H.M.s were the "Marthas," who served on committees, prepared the musical, dramatic, and fine arts components of the Congress, and provided clerical assistance. During the actual week of the Congress, in addition to giving presentations, the sisters gave hours of service in the sacristies, press rooms, and in hospitality lounges in airports, railway stations, and hotels. They served as special hostesses to the visiting clergy and guest speakers, as interpreters for bishops from foreign countries, and as marshals in the various processions.

In the various special liturgies for Hispanics, blacks, Ecumenical groups, senior citizens, Charismatics, and boy scouts, the sisters were found serving, and they were prominent at activities for the blind, retarded, and handicapped, assisting in any way they could. Especially in the program of Friday August 6, Youth Day, the Sisters of I.H.M. played a significant role.

As a result, many participants in the congress later sent messages commenting on the community spirit which they had observed, verifying the words which Father Gillet had written more than a hundred years before: "The brightly glowing flame of your community spirit is not only a glory to God but a source from which others may draw light and comfort. . . . For better or worse, you influence every soul with whom you come in contact."[29]

For weeks after the closing of the congress, letters were received from bishops, priests, religious, and members of the laity who had observed the sisters during the sessions and felt constrained to comment on their spirit. Bishop James Killeen from the Military Ordinariate in New York expressed his sentiments thus:

> Dear Mother Claudia:
> I feel sure that I will be only one of hundreds of priests and bishops to write to you praising your nuns for the gracious services they provided during the Eucharistic Congress. . . .
>
> Your sisters at the Congress, most of whom I saw doing sacristy work, were radiant with the spirit of joy. It would not be in any way out of order to say that they were in themselves a form of Eucharist. They showed the spirit of the love of God in their lives and they contributed in a large measure to making the Eucharistic Congress the most memorable spiritual experience of my life.[30]

From San Diego, Bishop Leo Maher wrote in a similar vein: " . . . our stay was also an inspirational one. Your community with its many members, great spirit, and dedication is most admirable."[31]

Not only from the United States, but also from Africa and Latin America came repercussions. Bishop R.S. Ndingi Mwana A. Nzeki of Nakuru, Kenya, visited Villa Maria during the Congress. As a result, he later had sisters from his diocese enroll at Immaculata College. In a letter of appreciation he stated, "Our sisters have all been impressed by the prevailing atmosphere of Christlike concern for others, and God's presence in your life and work."[32] The Bishop of Antofogasta in Chile declared: "During my stay in Philadelphia on the occasion of the forty-first International Eucharistic Congress, I had the opportunity of seeing many religious of your congregation. The 'Blue' religious were present in all places. I could observe their religious deportment, their dignified attitude, and many qualities which appeared in all the religious of your congregation with whom I had contact. I liked your congregation . . . "[33] He ended by requesting that the I.H.M.s establish a foundation in Antofogasta, but reluctantly the invitation was declined.

Various priests and religious touched upon the same characteristics, describing the spirit as one "which clearly shows itself in the faces and actions of your sisters and also in the obvious joy of your novices,"[34] "the spirit of joy and delight they radiated in whatever task they happened to be doing."[35] One priest who had not attended the Congress himself relayed some remarks which a group of religious of another community made to him upon their return, citing the presence of the I.H.M.s and their outstanding spirit,[36] while a local cleric characterized the sisters as "dedicated women, devoted and obviously in love with their Eucharistic Lord."[37] Noting that he and legions of others had watched the sisters work long hours sometimes with difficulty, behind the scenes, he did not hesitate to state that in his opinion without them the Congress would not have been the success it was.

The most unique comment was that of Joseph O'Hare in *America* who wrote:

> Many more young lively religious sisters were in evidence than the doomsayers would have thought possible. In fact, one cynic from Chicago suggested that dozens of airline stewardesses, well-scrubbed for the occasion, had been hired by the Congress committees to give religious vocations a brighter image. But no, inquiry revealed that they were all genuine, most of

them it seemed, from two Philadelphia-based communities, Sisters of Mercy and Sisters of the Immaculate Heart of Mary. Their fresh faces and enthusiasm as they swept down the aisles of the massive exhibit hall and sang at the massive liturgies were only one reminder among many of how much the joyous spirit of the Congress was due to the large number of young people, sisters, seminarians, and students who were present each day.[38]

Care of the Aged and Infirm

In the description of common life[39] the bishops exhorted religious to "give pride of place in esteem to each other and bear each other's burdens. For the community, a true family gathered together in the name of the Lord by God's love ... rejoices because He is present among them."

One of the surest evidences of a strong and loving community life is the care given to those sisters whom the Lord has visited with the cross of illness and suffering, and likewise to those reaching the end of lives spent in zealous labor in the apostolate. This has always been a high priortiy for this community and June 1960 marked the realization of a cherished dream when Camilla Hall was opened, a modern, three hundred-bed facility, located on the 375 acre campus at Immaculata. This replaced the infirmary in Wernersville, Pennsylvania which was becoming inadequate for the number who needed health care and which was not conveniently located for relatives and sisters who desired to visit the patients.

A chapel with a capacity of five hundred is the center of Camilla Hall where the Eucharistic Lord is exposed for adoration. Galleries are located on the second and third level to accommodate patients confined to wheelchairs, and a public address system carries to the rooms of the bedridden the daily liturgies. On each floor there are bright, attractive solariums where sisters who are unable to go to the main dining room gather for meals and recreation.

Two resident chaplains minister to the spiritual needs of the sisters, while the physical needs are met by dedicated physicians, nurses, licensed practical nurses, physical therapists, and dietitians, both religious and lay. Through the years the congregation has had sisters being prepared professionally as R.N.s, L.P.N.s, physical therapists, dietitians; currently one is being trained as a pharmacist. Thus, the residents not only have the advantage of modern equipment but also of qualified personnel.

In August 1967, application was made to the Commonwealth of Pennsylvania for certification as a health care facility; a certificate[40] was issued on April 4, 1968, subsequent to visitations and inspections conducted by Mrs. Helen Metz, Mrs. Poppert, Miss Glascow, representatives of the Pennsylvania Department of Health, and Mrs. Mootz, a federal inspector for Medicare.

In their statements on poverty, the bishops noted, "The several provinces and houses of each community should share their temporal goods with one another so that those who have more help the others who are in need."[41] During these years under consideration through the prudence and foresight of the treasurers of the congregation, Sister Marie Genevieve Lawler (now mother general) and her successor, Sister Eunice Marie Timoney, a special fund was established to provide for the upkeep of Camilla Hall and the needs of the sick and retired sisters. Serious study was given to the determination of an adequate endowment figure and at the annual meeting of the local superiors this was communicated and relayed to the congregation. Through simplicity of life-style, the various convents have been able to contribute annually to the fund. Moreover, individual members, in place of gifts for their personal use, welcome donations from relatives and benefactors as a continuing method of building up this fund.

More important, it has been the practice that the sisters involved in the active apostolate volunteer for service at Camilla on weekends and during vacation periods, thus displaying the real spirit of common life: giving not only of material resources but truly giving of themselves. On the other hand, these sisters appreciate the fact that their labors in the active apostolate are greatly furthered by the constant intercession of the sisters at Camilla, which is referred to as a "Powerhouse of Prayer." When Col. John F. Denehy learned of Camilla Hall and the loving care extended there he expressed in clear terms the mutual benefits derived:

> It is so definitely encouraging to find a community of our sisters who find absolute delight in caring for their aged and infirm community members not out of pure theological charity but in terms of truly invaluable assistance which the prayers and suffering of these aged and infirm members render to the community itself, its spiritual life and health, and the implementation of the similarly aged but no less invaluable corporal and spiritual works of mercy.[42]

CHAPTER VI

Sharing of Witness: Collaboration with Other Religious

Because the bishops of Vatican II believed firmly that true adaptation and renewal depended "greatly on the education of religious,"[1] they specified that religious should not be employed in apostolic work in the period immediately following the novitiate but rather profit from continued apostolic and religious formation, together with instruction in arts and sciences, as well as in the currents of thought and attitudes prevalent in social life today. This education by blending harmoniously the various elements would, in the opinion of the bishops, result in an integrated life.

Appropriate norms for the implementation of the decree, *Perfectae Caritatis*, were issued by Pope Paul VI and declared effective October 11, 1966, by way of experiment. In the document, *Ecclesiae Sanctae*, further elaboration on the training of religious recommended collaboration of several institutes as a means of providing opportunities which a single congregation would be unable to procure.[2] The Sisters of I.H.M. have participated in such joint undertakings through the years in two ways; first, through participation in organizations of woman religious, both national and international; second, by collaboration with specific religious communities.

Collaboration within Organizations

The need for, and the advantages of, collaboration had been noted even before Vatican II. As early as November 1950 a congress for Religious had been held in Rome. In 1952 Pope Pius XII had approved the International Congress of Superiors General of Orders and Congregations of Women Religious, which was summoned by the Sacred Congregation for Religious.[3] In the United States, the first national congress of religious was held at the University of Notre Dame, August 9–12, 1952, under the auspices of the Sacred Congregation for Religious. The purpose of the congress was threefold: 1) To serve as a means of intensifying and strengthening religious life in the United States; 2) To give religious of all institutes an opportunity to exchange ideas; and, 3) To discuss problems concerning the adjustment of religious life to conditions prevailing in the United States without compromising the principles on which religious life is built.[4] The congress was divided into two sections, and the one for women religious was presided over by Mother Mary Gerald Barry, O.P.

Cardinal Valeri, the prefect of the Sacred Congregation for Religious, had earnestly proposed the formation of an organization that would bring together the major superiors of women's communities to discuss problems common to all.[5] Therefore, on November 24, 1956, an organizational meeting was held in Chicago, arranged by Mother Gerald Barry, O.P., at which statutes for the body, henceforth to be called the Conference of Major Superiors of Women Religious, were adopted.

The first regular meeting was held in 1957. During her twelve years as superior general, Mother Maria Pacis participated actively by attending annual meetings. In 1961 she was elected chairman of the Eastern Region, and reelected in 1964.[6] Regional groups of this organization had been formed since experience showed that an annual meeting was not adequate for satisfactory treatment of all topics of concern.

Mother Claudia played a significant role in the activities of Region III, especially during her term as chairman (1971–74), specifically in her efforts to make the documents of Vatican II more clearly understood and appreciated by the membership.[7] Shortly after the publication of *Evangelica Testificatio*, Region III met at Villa Maria January 8, 1972 for a session at which Rev. Jude Mead, C.P., a counsultor to the Sacred Congregation for Religious and Secular Institutes, discussed this document. On August 28, of that same year Archbishop Augustin Mayer, O.S.B., the secretary of the S.C.R.S.I., offered the Eucharistic Liturgy at the I.H.M. Motherhouse and met with major superiors. Practically every congregation in Region III was represented.

Mother Claudia was also elected official representative to the national board, and in that capacity was named a member of the liaison committee with the National Conference of Catholic Bishops.[8]

On the national level changes were taking place that led to a revision of the statutes which had been approved by Rome in 1962. By 1970 the draft of the new statutes was presented, drastically altering the basic concepts of the former.[9] With the adoption of these bylaws in 1971, the C.M.S.W. went out of existence and the Leadership Conference of Women Religious took its place in 1972.

On October 13, 1970 a group of six major superiors

met at Villa Maria, Immaculata to continue a discussion they had begun a few weeks earlier at the annual meeting of the C.M.S.W. Present were Mother Maria Assumpta, S.S.J., Watertown, N.Y.; Mother Alice Anita, S.S.J., Chestnut Hill, Pa.; Mother Marie William, O.P., Nashville, Ten.; Mother Mary Elise, S.N.D., Chardon, Oh.; Mother Arthur Mary, S.N.D., Toledo, Oh.;[10] and Mother M. Claudia, I.H.M., Immaculata, Pa. Rev. Patrick Murray, S.J., was present as an advisor. At the end of the session they had reached an agreement that it would be mutually beneficial to invite other major superiors to join with them in forming a group for the purpose of communicating and sharing their experiences in implementing not only the documents of Vatican II regarding religious life, but also the subsequent papal statements, interpretations, and directives.

After another preliminary meeting[11] at the motherhouse of the Sisters of Saint Joseph, Watertown, New York, the process of contacting major superiors and bishops was continued, and by December 2, 1970, it was possible to convene a meeting at Chardon, Ohio, the provincialate of the Sisters of Notre Dame. This meeting was attended by sixty religious women, including major superiors, councilors, and formation personnel who represented thousands of sisters from various sections of the United States. Providentially, Cardinal Vagnozzi was visiting in this country at the time and he accepted the invitation to represent the Holy See. Bishops Elwell and Issenmann from Ohio were present and thirty other members of the hierarchy sent messages of support for the group. At this meeting the name *Consortium Perfectae Caritatis* was officially adopted. The pro-tempore national director of vocations, Reverened James Viall, was also in attendance, and he has through subsequent years given generously of his time and talents as a spiritual advisor to the group. Reverend John A. Hardon, S.J., has also served as its theological consultant.

In a letter to the Sisters, Servants of the Immaculate Heart of Mary, on March 25, 1971, Mother Claudia noted: "Consortium members are also members of the Conference of Major Superiors of Women, and hope to strengthen by mutual sharing the bonds of all those working for the continued holiness of the Church and religious congregations."

The major activity of this group during the ensuing years has been to arrange semiannual assemblies held in major cities of the U.S. at which speakers of international distinction have elucidated the teaching of Vatican II and principles of religious life. Among the lecturers have been more than forty cardinals and bishops coming from Italy, England, Ireland, France, and Poland, as well as the United States; from the ranks of religious and laity there have been outstanding theologians, historians, philosophers, sociologists, political scientists, and distinguished spiritual writers.[12]

Though it is not feasible to list all these by name, it may be of interest to note that Cardinal Ciappi, who addressed the group in November 1978, stated that he was probably the only speaker who ever had permission from three successive Popes to address an assembly. Since he was the Holy Father's personal theologian, he had requested permission from Pope Paul VI when the assembly was in the planning stages, subsequently from Pope John Paul I, and finally, from the present Holy Father before it actually took place in November.

While all the members of the institutes profited from the published proceedings, those in attendance at the assemblies had the added advantage of discussing with the other participants the implementation of the seven points upon which the members of the Consortium stand united; namely, they:

1—are convinced that the pursuit of holiness is the basic essential in the practice of the evangelical counsels;
2—stand in evident support of the Holy See and its right to interpret the norms of religious life for the Universal Church and the local churches;
3—believe in a permanent ecclesial commitment by vow to a corporate apostolate under the guidance of the hierarchy;
4—are responsive to the Roman Pontiff and his authority as exercised through the congregations established to assist him in the government of the Church;
5—live in a Eucharistic Community under the duly chosen superiors;
6—witness their consecration to God and their commitment to the world by the vow of poverty which prescribes the wearing of a distinctive religious habit;
7—live daily a community life within the program of communal prayer.

The Consortium had no officers but operated under an Administrative Council of Sisters, along with a spiritual advisor, a coordinator and a theological consultant, and was incorporated in the District of Columbia. As early as August 1972, it has been recognized by the Sacred Congregation for Religious and Secular Institutes in Rome when Cardinal Antoniutti, then prefect of the Congregation, issued a *Decretum Laudis*, and later Cardinal Ciappi expressed verbally the approval and benediction of Pope Paul VI, John Paul I, and John Paul II.[13]

Another group came into being in 1974 at the request

of the Sacred Congregation for Religious as a direct result of growing concern among bishops, priests, religious, and laity regarding the spiritual crisis in the modern world and its consequent effect on religious communities and their apostolic work. This national service organization, the Institute on Religious Life, was established to foster a more effective understanding and implementation of the teachings of the Magisterium of the Church. The Institute has pursued this purpose through study and research, consultation and counsel, and through the communication of official Church teaching on religious life.[14]

Among its many contributions, perhaps the most valuable is the publication *Consecrated Life*, a translation of the Vatican publication *Informationes*, through which the Sacred Congregation for Religious and Secular Institutes communicates to religious throughout the world. It contains statements of the Holy Father pertinent to religious life, decisions and decrees of the Holy See, important documents and studies, statistical information, and a current chronicle of the more important happenings regarding religious life and the activities of the Sacred Congregation. Since the Vatican edition is composed principally in Italian, but contains sections in other languages, notably German and French, the Institute has rendered a most welcome service to English-speaking religious throughout the world. A former president of the Institute on Religious Life, Cardinal Carberry, noted: "The publication is of historic importance for it makes available to all English-speaking religious and those concerned with religious life timely information about the activities, decisions, and guidelines of the Sacred Congregation . . . [and] labors for the strengthening and renewal of religious congregations and secular institutes in the contemporary world."[15]

From its inception, the Sisters, Servants of the Immaculate Heart of Mary have welcomed the opportunity to participate in this organization and to enjoy its benefits. Mother M. Claudia, then superior general, was elected at the first meeting, in December 1974, vice-president and has continued to serve on the board of directors to the present, while Mother Marie Genevieve is currently filling the office of vice-president. Many sisters have attended the annual meetings, and some have made presentations. Sister Clare Immaculate also served for a period as assistant secretary of the Institute.

On the international level, Mother Claudia was appointed in 1973 by the Sacred Congregation of Religious and Secular Institutes to the general council of the International Union of Superiors General (I.U.S.G.) for a term of three years.[16]

The I.U.S.G. was established by the Sacred Congregation on December 8, 1965. This organization of pontifical right unites the superiors general of congregations of religious women throughout the world through collaboration, sharing, and mutual support, in order to promote a continuous renewal of religious life in accordance with the mind of the church.

The general council (formed by the executive council and thirty general councilors chosen from different countries in such a way that it represents the religious institutes of the entire Church) meets in Rome at regular intervals to coordinate, implement, and stimulate the various activities according to the directives of the general assembly. The United States, because of the number of motherhouses of women religious, is entitled to two delegates elected by the L.C.W.R. and a third appointed by the Sacred Congregation. Mother Marie Genevieve[17] is currently serving a term of three years having been appointed by the Sacred Congregation in May 1983.

Collaboration with Individual Congregations

In these years since Vatican II, through cooperation with specific communities, the I.H.M.s have endeavored to comply with the council mandate: " . . . since all institutes are not able to impart in a satisfactory manner a doctrinal and technical formation, they can make up for this by fraternal collaboration. . . . The institutes which are well-provided as regards means of training, should be willing to help other institutes."[18]

On November 15, 1963, Archbishop Harold W. Henry of Kwanju, Korea, while he was in Rome for the Council, initiated correspondence with Mother Maria Pacis, mother general, requesting the admission of two members of the Caritas Community to the formation program of the Immaculate Heart Community.[19] This congregaton, founded in Myasaki, Japan, in 1938 by a Salesian missionary from Italy, Rev. Antonio Carrorri, was established in Korea by Archbishop Henry in Otober 1956. Within the first decade of its existence there, it numbered thirty-seven professed members, with forty in formation, and a promising number seeking admission. At the time of the Archbishop's request the Korean Sisters were doing missionary work in four parishes, providing education for the noninfected children of leper parents on Sorock Island, and conducting home economics classes for adults.[20] It was the hope of the archbishop that the sisters trained with the novices and junior sisters at Immaculata would return to Korea imbued with the spirit he saw among them and communicate it to the other members.[21]

On July 15, 1964, Sister Veronica Duk Hee Rhee and Sister Scholastica Mi Ae Rye took up residence in the novitiate of the Sisters, Servants of the Immaculate Heart of Mary. Since that day, the Caritas sisters from Korea and

Japan have shared in the religious formation and the educational programs of the Sisters of I.H.M. attaining the baccalaureate degree from Immaculata College before returning to convents in their native lands. Strong bonds have been forged, for both the host community and the visitors benefited from this sharing.

Representatives of an Italian congregation, the Comboni Missionary Sisters,[22] have shared the life not of novices and juniors, but of the aged and infirm, living at Camilla Hall while they received their collegiate education at Immaculata. In 1963 Mother Maria Pacis welcomed these sisters and throughout the subsequent years at least two members of that community have been on the campus, eventually leaving after graduation for Africa, Latin America, and Italy, as well as various sections of the United States.

This congregation was founded in Verona, Italy, in 1872 by Daniel Comboni, with evangelization for an apostolate, particularly in Africa. In very diverse ways they have pursued this goal; for example, by conducting schools in Ethiopia, a leprosarium in Uganda, and orphanages in the United States. Sister Dolores Smith, an Immaculata graduate, served as dean of studies in the university that the congregation operated in Ethiopia until 1982, when the government suppressed the institution.[23]

In 1972,[24] as a preparation for establishing a juniorate program at their provincialate in Mendham, New Jersey, the Sisters of Christian Charity arranged for their junior sisters to spend a year at Villa Maria House of Studies, sharing the facilities and formation courses there, while atttending Immaculata College for their academic preparation. Sister Julitta, S.C.C., who served as directress of juniors for the group, continued their formation in the special charism of their congregation.

On the Immaculata campus, sharing community life

with another segment of I.H.M.s, the sister faculty members, some Little Sisters of Saint Francis for Uganda have completed the baccalaureate program at the college.[25] Their congregation, founded in 1923 by a missionary from Ireland, Mother Kevin, now numbers almost four hundred members. These sisters labor in Uganda schools, hospitals, and orphanages. They conduct C.C.D. classes for the blind and operate homes for the elderly and disabled.[26]

More recently, a member of the Sisters of Saint Joseph from Kenya has been welcomed at the Immaculata community. This congregation, founded forty-five years ago by Sister Amedea (Precious Blood) and the Bishop of Mombasa, Kenya, conducts schools and C.C.D. classes in Kenya.[27] Although the membership is less than 150, the sisters also serve the sick and orphans.

Since the beginning of Vatican II, the Sisters, Servants of the Immaculate Heart have assisted in the formation of 120 sisters, representing 18 religious congregations.[28] This sharing has been inspired by the words of the Council Fathers: "The institutes which are well-provided as regards means of training should be willing to help other institutes."[29] However, it must be pointed out that this exchange has been mutually beneficial since the Immaculate Heart Sisters have been greatly enriched by the contact with these zealous religious, and have gained an added appreciation of the global ministry of the Church. It has been said: "Give a man a fish and he will eat for a day; teach him how to fish and he will eat for a lifetime." By assisting in training religious for service on continents where they themselves do not serve, the sisters feel deeply involved with young Catholics who, on the other side of the world, are being taught about Christ and being formed in His image. As the great Jesuit educator Father Daniel Lord once said: "The great—and would it be too much to say—

the sole task of Catholic education is simply this—the formation of other Christs. Christ came not to teach us how to die merely, but to teach us how to live, and there is no way of Christian living except in imitation of Christ, the Son of God, and the most perfect of men. Into the hands of his religious teachers Christ has given the most glorious of assignments—the task of helping others to grow in the fullness of the Christlike image and the completeness of the Christlike life."[30] By helping to train sisters who later go to the lepers of Korea, the pagans of Uganda, or the needy in Brazil, the Sisters of I.H.M. feel that they touch these souls vicariously.

When Archbishop Henry, back in 1963, began negotiating for the Caritas Sisters to come to Immaculata, he confided to Father Coulter his hope that in the future these sisters could pass on to others the admirable training they would receive there.[31] Five years later he wrote: "Sisters Veronica and Scholastica were very enthusiastic in their praise of your community . . . they also tell me of the tremendous spirit of charity and interest your sisters have in others. Well, this has rubbed off on them and I told them to be sure to bring this same spirit back to Korea."[32] In light of these statements, it is interesting to note that in four of these congregations mentioned above, the Comboni missionaries, the Caritas in Korea, the Caritas in Japan, and the Little Sisters of Saint Francis for Uganda, Africa, some of the sisters who shared formation at Immaculata later served as directresses of formation in their own respective congregations.

Of all these collaborative efforts, one is unique. It began with a request from Bishop Glennon Flavin of Lincoln, Nebraska, to Mother Claudia for assistance with a project he was about to undertake. His plan stemmed from his concern to have religious teachers in the diocesan schools as instruments to build up the body of Christ in the diocese.[33] Convinced of the necessity for such religious, he determined to found a congregation with education in the Catholic schools as their apostolate, and name them School Sisters of Christ the King. Once he had formed this resolution, there remained the necessity of finding an appropriate existing congregation willing to undertake the task of forming the new community. He singled out the Sisters, Servants of the Immaculate Heart of Mary.

This request was a most unexpected one in a year of much uncertainty regarding religious life. Just a few months earlier, one article in *Review for Religious* stated: " . . . the last fifteen to twenty years have been a time when most religious communities have begun to experience breakdown."[34] Bishop Flavin, however, believed that in the area of Lincoln there were young women ready to dedicate their lives to Christ.

Southern Nebraska had through the years a significant number of young women who accepted the call of Christ to dedicate themselves to vowed Christian living, and the percentage in relation to the total female population of the diocese is probably one of the highest in the nation. However, there had been a dramatic decrease in the number entering the convent in the sixties and seventies. From the historical perspective it must be attributed in part to the egocentric philosophy prevalent in the society of the day.[35] This search for "personal identity and fulfillment," with all its concentration on self, was not conducive to fostering in young people the spirit of self-sacrificing love through which Catholic schools had been established. Thoroughly convinced that "the Catholic school retains its immense importance[36] in the circumstances of our times," Bishop Flavin had made the courageous decision to gather together young women who wished to be faithful to the Holy

Father and the teachings of the Church, and who desired to spread the love of Christ to others.

Mother Claudia, with the assent of Cardinal Krol,[37] agreed to assist the new community by receiving interested candidates into the motherhouse at Villa Maria, Immaculata, Pennsylvania, for their religious and academic training. On September 12, 1976, three pioneers, Barbara Keese, Laurie Tobin, and Carol Raun began their preparation for religious life. During the term of their postulancy, Bishop Flavin continued his planning. It was decided that the sisters would wear a blue habit, similar to that of the Immaculate Heart Sisters, and a blue veil. In consultation with Mother Claudia and religious from the diocese of Lincoln[38] he formulated the constitutions titled, *Entrance into the Kingdom*. The statement regarding the spirit of the new group is: "Ardent love and zeal for teaching the Word of God, loyalty to the Church which is the Kingdom on earth, and devotion to the Blessed Sacrament will characterize the School Sisters of Christ the King. At all times they will give witness to loving fidelity to the Vicar of Christ, the Bishop, and the proper ecclesiastical authorities."[39]

On May 3,[40] Barbara and Laurie petitioned Mother Claudia and the council to receive the habit and to be admitted into the congregation of School Sisters of Christ the King. At the reception ceremony on June 26, 1977 in the Villa Maria chapel[41] they received the names Sister Rose James and Sister Joan Paul. Fittingly, Rev. Leonard Kalin, director of vocations for the diocese of Lincoln, presided at the ceremony, since he had supported and directed these candidates all along the way. Before Bishop Flavin formally requested the cooperation of the Immaculate Heart Sisters, Father Kalin had brought a vanload of students from the Newman Club of University of Nebraska to Villa Maria for a celebration of Eucharist and a visit with the novices and postulants.

In accordance with their constitutions, the sisters completed their novitiate training, devoting the first year to the study of theology and sacred sciences and the second year to additional doctrinal studies supplemented by courses designed for professional training.[42] Finally, on June 29, 1979, the two charter members traveled to Lincoln to prepare for the public profession of their vows which they made the following day in the Cathedral of the Risen Christ. In the name of the Church, Bishop Flavin received their vows.[43]

In preparation for the time when the School Sisters of Christ the King would be ready to begin their apostolate in Lincoln, Nebraska, the Sisters of I.H.M. agreed to staff a school in the newly formed parish of Saint Joseph.[44] Meanwhile, Sister Joan Paul gained experience in a well-established I.H.M. school, Our Lady of Charity, Brookhaven, Pennsylvania,[45] and Sister Rose James continued her studies at Immaculata College. As noted above, Saint Joseph school would at its inception begin with only grades kindergarten through three, since the sisters wished to have it permeated with their spirit and philosophy of education, to insure that it would provide a truly Christian atmosphere.[46]

The Sisters of the Immaculate Heart made an agreement[47] with Bishop Flavin which stated in part, "The Community will for an interval period, within the limitations of personnel and priorities, assign qualified sisters who, in cooperation with lay teachers employed by the parish, will staff the school. . . . Arrangements for the gradual replacement of Sisters of I.H.M. by School Sisters of Christ the King will be made, and in entering into the final decision to withdraw from the school the Major Superior will consult with the Ordinary of the diocese, the Superintendent of Schools and the Pastors."

On the occasion of the profession of these first members, Mother Claudia noted that towering over the city of Lincoln, atop the state Capital, is the figure of a man, his arms outstretched, sowing grain for the nation. The Great Plains have been called the bread basket of this land. In a letter to the Sisters, Servants of the Immaculate Heart of Mary, she stated: "It seemed that there the Divine Sower had been busy sowing the seeds of spiritual grain . . . Saturday, June 30, marked for the diocese of Lincoln and for the I.H.M.s the first ecclesial growth of a new diocesan community, a seed entrusted to us for nurturing, cast into the ground of I.H.M. formation and on this historic day bringing forth the fruit of the public profession of the first two School Sisters of Christ the King."[48]

Gradually other candidates presented themselves and at the end of its first decade of existence the community consisted of ten professed members, five novices, and three postulants. The Sisters of the I.H.M. had accepted[49] a second school in Lincoln, Saint Mary's in the Old Cathedral parish, and the staffing pattern was similar to that at Saint Joseph's. Currently, four of the School Sisters of Christ the King are teaching at Saint Joseph's and three at Saint Mary's, while the remainder are continuing their studies.

In 1983 Bishop Flavin began to implement his desire to have the formation program based in Lincoln. To provide suitable facilities during an interim period before a permanent motherhouse would be established, Bishop Flavin sought special permission from the City Council of Lincoln[50] for the construction of temporary facilities in that city.[51] Villa Regina Religious Formation Center, erected on a seventeen acre site formerly owned by the American Conference Association of the Seventh Day Adventist Church, was completed in August 1984. The first community consisted of Sister Joseph Fidelis Dorwart, I.H.M., superior, Sister Regina Marion Copple, I.H.M., directress of formation, and the sister faculty members of both Saint Joseph and Saint Mary schools. Included in the group were Sister Jude Mary O'Donnell, I.H.M., Sister John Evelyn DiTrolio, I.H.M., Sister Anne Joelle Braunsroth, S.S.C.K., Sister Anne Mathias Beckius, S.S.C.K., Sister Christopher Mary Stall, S.S.C.K., Sister Joan Paul Tobin, S.S.C.K., Sister Rose James Keese, S.S.C.K., and Sister Patrick Elizabeth O'Meara, S.S.C.K.[52]

On September 24, three postulants entered, Christine Linscott, Julie Keashall, and Jean Marie Besch.[53] Since Bishop Flavin had urgently requested the Sisters of the I.H.M. to continue to direct the formation program, Sister Regina Marion was assigned as the first directress in the Lincoln motherhouse. During the first year, courses in Sacred Scripture, theology, church music, and philosophy were conducted by Rev. Myron Pleskac, Rev. James Divis, Rev. Cornelius Holly, and Sister Mary Durr, O.P.[54]

On August 15, 1985, these three postulants received their habits and were admitted to the novitiate as Sister Mary Alma, Sister Mary Michael, and Sister Mary Celeste. With the admission of three additional postulants in September 1986, the new formation program was under way.[55] One of the professors who participated in the initial years of the program reported that, in his opinion, the venture shows great promise.[56]

In collaborating with Bishop Flavin in this project, the Sisters of the Immaculate Heart of Mary furthered the realization of the dream of their own Founder, Father Gillet. More than a century earlier he had labored to establish in the Midwest schools conducted by religious, because he perceived this as the most effective way of preserving the Catholic faith. Thus in the spirit of their Founder, the sisters willingly contributed time, energy, and resources to respond to the call of the bishops of Vatican II, who had enunciated the principle: "... when individual institutes cannot give adequate doctrinal or technical training this can be provided by the fraternal collaboration.... Institutes equipped with the necessary means should willingly assist others."[57]

CHAPTER VII

Facets of Witness: Liturgical Prayer

Vatican Council II set out "to impart an ever-increasing vigor to the Christian life of the faithful ... and to strengthen whatever can help to call all mankind into the Church's fold."[1] The first document published was that on the liturgy, since it is, in the words of the Council Fathers, "through the liturgy especially that the faithful are enabled to express in their lives and manifest to others the mystery of Christ and the real nature of the true Church."

The response to this document on the part of the sisters has two aspects. First, there is the educational and attitudinal formation of each individual sister through her experiences in liturgical prayer life. As each sister deepens her own spirituality, there is an effect on the congregation's sense of worship, sense of personal prayer and contemplation, and ultimately on the congregation's distinctive spirituality. Second, as educators, there is the effort to instruct others in a proper understanding of the changes made by the Council, and of participating with them in inspiring and reverent liturgies. The Sacred Congregation on Rites called religious "to draw from [the liturgy] nourishment both for their own spiritual lives and for communication to others" in their subsequent labors.[2]

The earliest efforts on the part of the congregation to respond to liturgical reforms recommended by Vatican II took the form of special study by a core group. They prepared the liturgies in those institutions where sisters in large numbers assembled during the summer months, i.e., Villa Maria-by-the-Sea, Immaculata College, and Villa Maria House of Studies. The participants were in turn prepared to plan liturgies in various local communities. Much assistance was given by Reverend John Miller, secretary of the Commission on Sacred Liturgy of the Archdiocese of Philadelphia, who gave a three-week workshop at Villa Maria House of Studies. Later, several one-day sessions on various aspects were offered.

During the scholastic year, as the sisters gathered daily for the Eucharistic Liturgy and the Liturgy of the Hours, there was a serious effort to plan for these. In March 1972, Sister Maureen Stephen Deller prepared a brochure giving guidelines for the Eucharistic Celebration which was distributed to all members of the congregation. Before distribution it was submitted to the Commission on Sacred Liturgy of the Archdiocese of Philadelphia for approval. The secretary responded as follows:

> May I say first of all that this paper is truly excellent. It is gratifying in the extreme to note so fine a knowledge of the directives of *The Rite of Mass* and so deep an appreciation of their purpose. I offer praise and thanks on behalf of the Liturgy Commission.
>
> When the paper is ready for distribution, may I have copies for the other members of the Commission? Even more useful, could copies be sent to the Superiors General or Provincials of all the Communities who serve in the Archdiocese? We are most interested in seeing such projects shared, and the

Commission will take care of this publication. The fact of one Community's completing such an initiative with such success would lend encouragement to others to enter upon similar projects.[3]

During the following year, musicians who had special training offered their assistance to the local communities.[4] One comment regarding the activities of the I.H.M.s in planning liturgies came from Reverend Lester H. Mitchell, O.F.M. After conducting a retreat, he wrote:

> During this month of June I directed a retreat for mixed communities of sisters at Saint Clare's Retreat... I was most impressed by the Sisters, Servants of the Immaculate Heart of Mary. Since there were a number of your community and all wore the same sharp-looking habit, it was easy to notice them ... their spirit captivated everyone—happy, fun-loving, very prayerful, friendly, immensely helpful. At this retreat house the sisters making the retreat form their own liturgical committee.... Several of your sisters willingly spearheaded the movement. They ended up by carrying generously most of the burden yet really encouraged other sisters and communities to get involved. I did not keep count of the sisters who would mention the fine spirit of your sisters, the fun in seeing such happy women ... I personally was so impressed with the kindness of your sisters, the happiness they showed, their marvelous, positive attitude ... it was a sincere and great pleasure to meet this community for the first time. With members like this you are a blessing to all the Church. Keep up this kind of witnessing—all of us must see such inspiration that reminds us constantly to "shape up."[5]

Another priest also was prompted to comment after conducting a retreat at Villa Maria. Reverend Jude Mead,

C.P., requested that the congregation allow some of the musicians, who were so well versed in the liturgical movement, to assist the Carmelite Sisters of the Aged and Infirm. Consequently, Sister Cecile Marie Phalen and Sister Maureen Stephen were invited to give a week's workshop at their monastery in Germantown, New York.

Through the years the congregation has offered sisters the opportunity to increase their knowledge in the area of sacred liturgy by inviting liturgical specialists to Immaculata and also by having sisters enroll for a second advanced degree in this field. So that every segment of the community would be reached, a specially trained musician was assigned full time to Camilla Hall, the home for the aged and infirm.

The initial attempt to involve and serve local parishes took the form of a workshop at Immaculata College in October 1977.[6] Interest on the part of faculty members in both the theology and music departments led to several projects over the next five years. They included workshops, seminars, lecture series, courses, and practicums. Among the liturgical specialists who lectured in these were representatives of several religious communities (Augustinians, Benedictines, and Premonstratensians), as well as members of the diocesan clergy. Sisters of the I.H.M. and members of the laity completed the faculty.

The objectives of this effort included both the educational and attitudinal formation of sisters through experiences in liturgical prayer life, and the effort to develop among the laity skills necessary to function as music ministers in a faith community. Finally, in 1983 approval was granted to establish at Immaculata College a certificate program in music and liturgy. This program has as its first goal: "To further the development of music and liturgy in keeping with standards of musical excellence and the norms and recommendations of the Constitution on Sacred Liturgy." During these earliest years the program has been received with much interest and gives promise of having a significant effect on the liturgical life of parishes in the area.

Sacred Art which is treated in a special section on the Constitution on the Sacred Liturgy was the subject of a week-long workshop at Immaculata College in 1985.

Fathers of the Council noted that "all artists who ... desire to serve God's glory in holy church should ever bear in mind that they are engaged in a kind of sacred imitation of God the Creator, and are concerned with works destined for use in Catholic worship and for the edification, devotion, and religious instruction of the faithful."[7]

Art works of Sisters, Servants of the Immaculate Heart of Mary are currently in the Saint Thomas More Cathedral in Arlington, Virginia, in the National Shrine of the Immaculate Conception in Washington, D.C., and in the State Capitol Museum in Harrisburg, Pennsylvania.

The metal repoussée of Bishop John Keating's seal which adorns the marble episcopal chair in the sanctuary of the Cathedral of Saint Thomas More in Arlington is the work of Sister Eileen Mary Mattis. In executing it, Sister used in connection with the metal, a transparent paint for the colored section of the seal. A similar reproduction of the seal of the founder of the diocese, Bishop Thomas Welsh, is also her handiwork and is preserved in the diocesan archives after its removal from the cathedral.

In the National Shrine of the Immaculate Conception in Washington, the life-size bronze of Saint Vincent Pallotti presented to the Shrine by the Pallottine Immaculate Conception province is the work of Sister Mary Paula Beierschmitt, I.H.M. When the Pallottine congregation decided to make such a presentation in observance of their

150th jubilee year, they commissioned Sister Paula, whose sculpture "The Handmaid" had been in the Marian exhibit sponsored by the Paul VI Institute for the Arts in 1982 when it received a second national award. Sister has declared that the raison d'être of her aesthetic endeavor is to retain integrity and a spiritual essence in the visual arts, whether the subject is sacred or secular. For this reason, she especially laments the saccharine sentimentality into which many religious works have declined.

Another of Sister's sculptures, that of Reverend Louis Florent Gillet, was awarded the first prize in the division of religious art in the Greater Harrisburg Arts Festival in March 1986. It is presently exhibited in the Pennsylvania State Museum in Harrisburg, Pennsylvania. In addition to the award in the religious art division, it was also selected for the second place sculpture award.

Sister is the only woman religious to hold a diploma from the Pennsylvania Academy of Fine Arts, America's oldest fine arts institute. Founded in 1805, it counts among its graduates Thomas Eakins and Mary Cassatt.

Sister Helen David Brancato has made several important contributions in the area of graphic arts. The Maryknoll Society commissioned her in the summer of 1986 to design Stations of the Cross based on the missionary spirit and currently the well-known spiritual writer, Reverend Henri Nouwen, is composing meditations to accompany them. The Maryknoll Fathers had previously tapped her expertise in 1985 and 1986 when she did the art work for their educational units on Central America and the Phillippines. Sister also did the art work for a volume prepared by the Catholic Relief Services in 1981, *Bread Broken for a New World*. This publication reached tens of thousands of students throughout the United States, and through it Sister extended her influence far beyond the students whom she daily inspires in her classes.

Immaculata College has been mentioned several times in these pages. The scope of this study does not permit a detailed treatment of the college's history during these decades, although it is hoped that one day that story will be written. In these troubled years when many small Catholic liberal arts colleges for women were unable to survive, Immaculata has prospered under the prudent and enlightened leadership of three successive presidents, Sister Mary of Lourdes McDevitt, Sister Marie Antoine Buggy, and Sister Marian William Hoban. It is the oldest Catholic women's college in the Philadelphia area.

Through the establishment of an evening division,[8] a graduate program, and several curricular additions on the undergraduate level, e.g., a music therapy and a baccalaureate program for R.N.s, the college has been able to maintain its enrollment both of traditional- and nontraditional-age students. Immaculata has retained through the years this goal: "Immaculata College, aware of the demands of a changing society, offers her students the means to grow as integral persons, responsible to God, the Church, and man, and stimulates them to realize this growth within a Christ-centered academic community."[9]

Conclusion

At the outset, this study was described as a reflection on some of the ways the congregation of the Sisters, Servants of the Immaculate Heart of Mary has developed since Vatican II. In the words of Archbishop Quinn, it was a review of experiences and structural changes in the light of the teaching of the Church on religious life and of the religious witness the sisters are giving in the American context.[10] While the work was in progress, Pope John Paul II summoned the extraordinary synod of 1985.

In his homily at the Eucharistic Liturgy which closed

the synod the Pope declared: "As we come out of the Synod, we wish to intensify our pastoral efforts to ensure that the Second Vatican Council is more widely and more thoroughly known; to ensure that the orientations and directives that the Council left us are assimilated into the very heart of all the members of the People of God and translated into the way they live with consistency and love."[11]

The years ahead will disclose how the Sisters, Servants of the Immaculate Heart of Mary respond to this demanding challenge of Christ's vicar.

Notes

Chapter 1. Call to Witness: Invitation of Vatican II

1. Robert J. Daly, S.J., ed., *Religious Life in United States Church*, (Ramsey, N.J., Paulist Press, 1984), 21.
2. Pope John XXIII, *Documents on Renewal for Religious*, (Boston, Mass.: Daughters of St. Paul, 1974), 15.
3. Ibid.
4. *Perfectae Caritatis*, 2.
5. *Evangelica Testificatio*, 51.
6. Rev. Elio Gambari, *Renewal in Religious Life*, (Boston, Mass., Daughters of St. Paul, 1967), 193.
7. Mother Marie Alma, *Sisters, Servants of the Immaculate Heart of Mary, 1845–1934* (Philadelphia, Pa., Dolphin Press, 1934), 72.
8. Thomas McDermott, *Keeper of the Keys*, (Milwaukee, Bruce Publishing Co., 1946), 125.
9. James F. Connelly, Ed., *The History of the Archdiocese of Philadelphia*. (Philadelphia, Archdiocese of Philadelphia, 1976), 466.
10. *L'Osservatore Romano*, 11/25/78.
11. Pope John Paul II, *Visible Signs of the Gospel*, (Boston, Mass., Daughters of St. Paul, 1980), 127.
12. Austin Flannery, O.P., Ed., *Vatican Council II, More Post Conciliar Documents*, (Northport, N.Y., Costello Publishing Co., 1982), 609, "the absence of the Catholic school would be a great loss for civilization and for the natural and supernatural destiny of man."
13. Villa Maria House of Studies Archives, Immaculata, PA. 19345. (Hereafter designated V.M.H.S. Archives) Letter from Bishop Thomas Welsh to Mother M. Claudia, April 1, 1981. Mother M. Claudia served as mother general of the Congregation from December 28, 1968 to June 27, 1981. For a list of mothers general and their councils (1945 to present) refer to Appendix A.
14. V.M.H.S. Archives. Letter from Bishop Joseph McShea to Mother M. Claudia, April 22, 1981.

15. V.M.H.S. Archives. Letter from Bishop Joseph Daley to Mother M. Claudia, April 15, 1981.
16. V.M.H.S. Archives. Letter form Archbishop Edward A. McCarthy to Mother M. Claudia, April 24, 1981.
17. V.M.H.S. Archives. Letter from Archbishop John F. Whealon to Mother M. Claudia, March 31, 1981.
18. V.M.H.S. Archives. Letter from Bishop Glennon Flavin to Mother M. Claudia, April 2, 1981.
19. V.M.H.S. Archives. Letter from Archbishop Joseph McGucken to Mother M. Claudia, March 30, 1981.
20. V.M.H.S. Archives. Letter from Archbishop John Quinn to Mother M. Claudia, April 29, 1981.
21. V.M.H.S. Archives. Letter from Bishop Pierre du Maine to Mother M. Claudia, June 17, 1981.
22. Letter to Bishops of U.S.A. June 19, 1976. *Social Justice Review*, August 1976, 110.
23. Actually, to the question "Should Catholic education be retained as the principal apostolate?" only 2 percent answered in the negative. The other 3 percent either failed to respond, or gave responses which the committee characterized as irrelevant.
24. *Faithful Witness*, 42–43.
25. V.M.H.S. Archives. Letter from Archbishop (now Cardinal) Augustin Mayer to Mother Marie Genevieve, April 26, 1983.

Chapter 2. Origin of Witness: Charism and Early History

1. Mother Maria Alma, *Sisters, Servants of the Immaculate Heart of Mary 1845–1967* (Lancaster, Pa., Dolphin Press, 1967).
2. Sister M. Immaculata, *The Sisters of the I.H.M.* (New York, P.J. Kennedy and Sons, 1921).
3. Sister M. Rosalita, *No Greater Service*, (Monroe, Sisters, Servants of the Immaculate Heart of Mary, 1948).
4. Robert Daly, S.J., op. cit. 112.
5. Sister Maria Alma, *The Reverend Louis Florent Gillet* (Philadelphia, Pa., Dolphin Press, 1940), 39.
6. Gillet to De Held, October 12, 1843 *Journal historique et litteraire*, XI (January, 1845), 487.
7. Sister M. Rosalita, op. cit., 29.
8. Rev. Louis Gillet, *Historical Account* (Original French in V.M.H.S. Archives).
9. "If I do not find a religious community, I shall organize one." Mother Maria Alma, *Sisters, Servants of the Immaculate Heart of Mary 1845–1967*, (Lancaster, Pennsylvania, Dolphin Press, 1967), 30.

10. Sister M. Celestine, *Historical Chronology of Our Community*. Manuscript in Monroe Motherhouse Archives, St. Mary's, Monroe, Michigan 48161.
11. Mother Maria Alma, *Thou, Lord, Art My Hope*, (Lancaster, Pa., Dolphin Press, 1944), 44.
12. Sister Maria Alma, *The Reverend Louis Florent Gillet*, 55.
13. The Monroe congregation possesses only a certified copy of the Bishop's letter of approval. Mother Theresa, on her departure for Pennsylvania on April 1, 1859, took letters, an English translation of the Chronicles, and a manuscript copy of the Rule. All of these were lost in a fire that destroyed St. Joseph College, in Susquehanna, on the night of January 1, 1864.
14. Monroe Motherhouse Chronicles.
15. Ibid.
16. Gillet to De Held, January 27, 1846. *Journal historique et litteraire*, XIII, 11.
17. Cf. Letter to Editor, January 2, 1845. *Catholic Herald* quoted in Sister Maria Alma, *The Reverend Louis Florent Gillet*, 45–46.
18. For the most detailed exposition of this incident, see Sister M. Rosalita, op. cit., 173–179.
19. Ibid, 77.
20. Monroe Motherhouse Archives. Smolders to Sisters, I.H.M., November 8, 1891.
21. Archdiocese of Detroit Archives. Ruland to LeFevre, March 17, 1854. The Provincial of the Redemptorists notified the Bishop of the withdrawal of the community from St. Mary's, Monroe.
22. Sister M. Rosalita, op. cit., 99.
23. Ibid., p. 79.
24. Scranton Motherhouse Archives. Mother Theresa's Notes.
25. Sister M. Rosalita, op. cit., 151.
26. Mother Maria Alma, *The Sisters, Servants of the Immaculate Heart of Mary, (1845–1967)*, 91.
27. Ibid., 145.
28. Ibid., 175.
29. University of Notre Dame Archives. De Held to LeFevre, November 4, 1847. Cf. also, Sister M. Rosalita, op. cit, 179–180.
30. Mount St. Alphonsus Archives, Esopus, New York 12429. Diary of Fr. Bernard Hafkenscheid, C.SS.R., January–March, 1849.
31. Sister M. Rosalita, op. cit., 181.
32. *The Catholic Telegraph*, January 12, 1850 (Cincinatti).
33. St. Joseph Seminary Archives, Dunwoodie, New York 10704. Hafkenscheid to Hughes, May, 1853, Copy in V.M.H.S. Archives.
34. *L'union Cistersienne*, December 1892. (Necrologie-Pere Celestin), copy in V.M.H.S. Archives.
35. Pere Marie Celestin, *Notice*, May 1891.

36. *Registre*, Notre Dame d'Hautecombe. Extract provided by Dom Marie Bernard, C.I.C. September 29, 1925.
37. Peter Marie Celestin, op. cit.
38. Annals of Senanque, 165.
39. *L'union Cistercienne*, loc. cit.
40. V.M.H.S. Archives. *Register, Sisters of I.H.M.*
41. Related by Sister M. Clotilde to Mother Maria Alma. cf *The Reverend Louis Florent Gillet*, 105.
42. Notre Dame de Pres.
43. V.M.H.S. Archives. Sister Marie Stephanie, Correspondence covering the period 1866–1908 (Original French).
44. Letter of March 27, 1888.
45. Father Cesaire. *cf*, Sister Marie Alma, *The Reverend Louis Florent Gillet*, 191.
46. December 25, 1890. Copy in V.M.H.S. Archives.
47. *National Catholic Directory*, 1892.
48. V.M.H.S. Archives. Original French manuscript referred to above as *Notice*.
49. V.M.H.S. Archives. Letter from Pere Marie Symphorien, Prior of Hautecombe, dated November 15, 1892.
50. Cf. *No Greater Service*, pp. 567–569 for details. At first the Cistercians, fearing the government under which they lived, sought to dissuade the Sisters, assuring them that even if the exhumation were permitted, nothing would remain, since a Cistercian's coffin is always made of the cheapest of soft woods, and since the body had been interred in damp earth on the shore of Lake Bourget thirty-three years before. However, at the time of the exhumation, the coffin, which by some exception had been made of hard wood, was found intact and only a few of the smaller bones of the skeleton had fallen into dust.
51. V.M.H.S. Archives. Original French.
52. *Perfectae Caritatis*, 2.
53. V.M.H.S. Archives. Original documents.
54. *Ecclesiae Sanctae*, 28.

Chapter 3. Extension of Witness: Apostolate

1. *Gravissimum Educationis*, 8. Walter M. Abbott, S.J. (ed.) *Documents of Vatican II*, (New York, America Press, 1966), 647.
2. *Gaudium et Spes*, 51.
3. *The Catholic High School: A National Portrait*, (Washington, D.C., N.C.E.A., 1985) p. 126. Statistics in the *National Catholic Directory* 1986 indicate a decline of less than 1 percent in Catholic educational institutions since 1985.
4. Robert Daly, S.J., Ed., op. cit. 164–5.

5. Ibid, 163.
6. *Athens Banner Herald*, April 24, 1969.
7. V.M.H.S. Archives. Letter from C.H. Edwards, President, Board of Education to Mother M. Claudia, January 30, 1970.
8. Dr. Helen Westbrook, representative of the association, visited the school on December 3, 1984.
9. V.M.H.S. Archives. Letter from Mother M. Claudia to Msgr. Richard Burke, Superintendent of Schools, Richmond, Va., April 9, 1969.
10. V.M.H.S. Archives. Letter from Rev. Thomas Quinlan to Mother M. Claudia, March 31, 1977.
11. V.M.H.S. Archives. Letter from Mother M. Claudia to Msgr. Francis Schulte, March 11, 1977.
12. V.M.H.S. Archives, 1985–86.
13. Mother Catherine Drexel made her vows February 12, 1891, as the first Sister of the Blessed Sacrament for Indians and Colored People. Sister Consuela Marie Duffy, *Katharine Drexel*, (Philadelphia: Peter Reilly Company, 1965), 169.
14. V.M.H.S. Archives. Letter from Msgr. Francis Schulte to Mother M. Claudia, March 31, 1973.
15. *Southern Nebraska Register*, December 16, 1983.
16. V.M.H.S. Archives. Letter from Rev. Michael A. Cupuano to Mother M. Claudia, April 8, 1979.
17. *The Intelligencer*, March 17, 1985.
18. V.M.H.S. Archives. Letter from Rev. William McKeever to Mother Maria Alma, March 27, 1953.
19. *Miami Herald*, September 6, 1981.
20. Robert Daly, S.J., op. cit. 164.
21. *Bucks County Courier Times*, June 3, 1969.
22. Ibid, March 7, 1970.
23. V.M.H.S. School Records.
24. Pope John Paul II at National Shrine, Washington, D.C., October 7, 1979. *U.S.A. The Message of Justice, Peace, and Love*, (Boston, Ma., Daughters of Saint Paul, 1979), 240.
25. *Southern Nebraska Register*, May 18, 1984.
26. V.M.H.S. Archives. Letter from Bishop George Guilfoyle to Mother Maris Pacis, December 20, 1968.
27. V.M.H.S. Archives. Letter from Mother M. Claudia to Msgr. Francis Barrett, April 27, 1972.
28. V.M.H.S. Archives. Annals, St. Joseph, Girardville.
29. V.M.H.S. Archives.
30. Mother Maria Alma, *Sisters, Servants of the Immaculate Heart of Mary 1845–1967*, 291.
31. V.M.H.S. Archives. School Book Records.
32. Lois Dougherty, *Evening Herald*, May 10, 1981.

33. V.M.H.S. Archives. Letter from Cardinal Dougherty to Mother M. Loyola, May 29, 1929.
34. January 23, 1977. Record in V.M.H.S. Archives.
35. V.M.H.S. Archives. Annals, Our Lady of Pompeii Convent, 1940.
36. V.M.H.S. Archives. Annals, St. Augustine, Bridgeport.
37. V.M.H.S. Archives. Annals, St. Cecilia, Coatesville.
38. V.M.H.S. Archives. Letter from Msgr. Francis Schulte to Mother M. Claudia, December 18, 1974.
39. V.M.H.S. Archives. Minutes of Meeting held at St. Gertrude's, October 11, 1976.
40. Public School Code of Pennsylvania 1361. When provision is made by a board of directors for the transportation of resident pupils to and from the public schools, the board of school directors shall also make identical provisions for the free transportation of pupils who regularly attend nonpublic elementary and high schools not operated for a profit. *See* Seventy-second Annual School Report, Archdiocese of Philadelphia, 1965–66, 11.
41. V.M.H.S. Archives. Minutes of Meeting held at St. Joseph.
42. V.M.H.S. Archives. Letter from Mother M. Claudia to Superintendent of Schools, April 1, 1980.
43. V.M.H.S. Archives. Minutes of Meeting, October 21, 1980.
44. *Supra*, p. 24.
45. V.M.H.S. Archives. Letter from Rev. Eugene Shellem to Mother Marie Genevieve, February 20, 1984.
46. p. 2.
47. V.M.H.S. School Records.
48. Mother Maria Alma, *Sisters, Servants of the Immaculate Heart of Mary*, 1845–1967, 389.
49. Ibid, 316–317.
50. Ad Gentes, 15. Austin Flannery, O.P., *Vatican Council II, The Counciliar and Post-Conciliar Documents*, (Collegeville, Mi., 1975), 831.
51. Sister Joseph Marie, *American Catholic Historical Society Records*. Vol. 53, March, 1942, 54–57.
52. V.M.H.S. Archives.
53. Chapter 2, page 20.
54. V.M.H.S. Archives. Letter from Father Nevin Hayes to Mother Maria Alma, March 20, 1955.
55. V.M.H.S. Archives, Letter from Fr. Francis Provenzano to Mother Maria Pacis, April 1, 1959.
56. V.M.H.S. Annals.
57. V.M.H.S. Archives. Letter from Sister Marie Arthur to Mother Marie Genevieve, September 18, 1984.
58. V.M.H.S. Archives. Letter from Mother Marie Genevieve to Sisters, Servants of the Immaculate Heart of Mary.
59. V.M.H.S. Archives. Letter from Rev. Henry B. Haske, S.J. to

Mother Maria Pacis, May 9, 1967.
60. Statement issued May 10, 1973. Copy in V.M.H.S. Archives.
61. *Evangelica Testificatio*, 39. *Documents on Renewal for Religious,* (Boston, Ma., Daughters of Saint Paul, 1974), 235–36.
62. Related by Rev. Francis Nugent, S.J. to Sister Margaret Mary, March, 4, 1986.
63. p. 46.
64. V.M.H.S. Archives. Letter from Bishop Lorenzo Alvarado to Mother M. Claudia, April 1, 1972.
65. V.M.H.S. Archives. Annals, San Ildephonso, Barranca.
66. Related by Sister Clare Mary, Regional Superior in Latin America, to Sister Margaret Mary, April 9, 1986.
67. V.M.H.S. Archives. Letter from Bishop Lorenzo Alvarado to Mother M. Claudia, April 1, 1972. The population of Barranco is 80,000.
68. *Ad Gentes*, 17. Abbott, op. cit., 605.
69. *Sacrosanctum Concilium*, 48. Ibid., 154.
70. *Gaudium et Spes*, 31. Ibid., 229.
71. V.M.H.S. Archives. School records.
72. Related by Sister Miriam Rose, former Regional Superior in Latin America to Sister Margaret Mary.
73. *Ad Gentes*, 1. Abbott, op. cit., 585.
74. Monroe Motherhouse Archives.
75. *Perfectae Caritatis*, 2.
76. V.M.H.S. Archives.
77. *Catechesi Tradendae*, (Boston, Ma., Daughters of Saint Paul), 65.
78. *Blackstone Courier Record*, July 18, 1974.
79. *Catholic Standard and Times*, August 9, 1973.
80. In 1973, Monsignor Teller, Director of C.C.D. estimated this number at 111,000.
81. V.M.H.S. Archives.
82. St. Lucy School was founded by Archbishop O'Hara in 1953. Mainstreaming, a common practice in 1986, was an unusual concept at the time of its founding.
83. V.M.H.S. Archives.
84. *Catechesi Tradendae*, op. cit, 62.

Chapter 4. Formation for Witness: Professional Preparation

1. *Perfectae Caritatis*, 18. Abbott, op. cit., 470.
2. Mother Maria Alma, *Sisters, Servants of the Immaculate Heart of Mary 1845–1967*, (Lancaster, Pa., Dolphin Press, 1967), 237.
3. Ibid, 247.

4. Catholic Historical Society of America Archives, St. Charles Seminary, Overbrook, Pa. 19151.
5. Final decree was endorsed by Judge Hause in the Court of Common Pleas, Chester Country, and filed there November 29, 1920.
6. "Pope Pius XII to Teaching Sisters," *Catholic Mind*, June, 1952, 376–80.
7. See Appendix D.
8. *To Teach As Jesus Did*, 103.
9. V.M.H.S. Archives.
10. St. Charles Seminary Archives.
11. Bulletin, St. Charles Seminary, Religious Studies Division.
12. *Sacrosanctum Consilium*, 6.
13. V.M.H.S. Archives. Educational Records.
14. St. Charles Seminary Archives.
15. V.M.H.S. Archives. Educational Records.
16. Report to General Chapter, 1974.
17. *Gravissimum Educationis*, 12. Abbott, op. cit., 651.
18. V.M.H.S. Archives. Minutes of General Chapter.
19. V.M.H.S. Archives. Educational Records.
20. Immaculata College Archives, Immaculata, Pa. 19345.
21. Sister M. Francilla O'Donnell and Sister Agnes Patrice Healey.
22. 1970.
23. Minutes, Board of Trustees, Immaculata College.
24. The program received approval from the Pennsylvania Department of Education, 1983.
25. Pope John Paul II, *U.S.A.—The Message of Justice, Peace, and Love*, (Boston: Daughters of St. Paul, 1979), 246.
26. Immaculata College Archives.
27. *Gravissimun Educationis*, 8. Abbot, op. cit. 647.
28. Sister Joseph Kieran McAdams. V.M.H.S. Archives, Educational Records.
29. *Ad Gentes*, 12. Abbott, op. cit. 589–99.
30. Chapter 3, pp. 45–55.
31. Immaculata College Archives.
32. V.M.H.S. Archives.
33. Immaculata College Archives.
34. V.M.H.S. Archives.
35. St. Charles Seminary records.
36. Immaculata College Archives.
37. V.M.H.S. Archives.
38. *Perfectae Caritatis*, 18. Abbott, op. cit., 470.
39. *Declaration on Christian Education*, 8. Flannery, op. cit., 733.

40. *Differentiated Supervision in Catholic Schools*, (Washington, N.C.E.A. 1983).
41. James J. Kilpatrick, *The Philadelphia Inquirer*, March 11, 1986.
42. *Catholic Schools*, 1, 8. Flannery, op. cit. 608.

Chapter 5. Exchange of Witness: Community Life and Spirit

1. *Perfectae Caritatis*, 15, *Documents on Renewal for Religious*, 85.
2. *Ibid.*
3. *Faithful Witness*, 27.
4. *John Paul II Speaks to Religious* (Chicago, IL, Little Sisters of the Poor), 261.
6. cf. *Ecclesiae Sanctae*, 21.
7. Pope Paul VI to Superiors General 1975.
8. *John Paul II Speaks to Religious*, p. 115, Address to the Superiors General of Religious Women in Rome, November 14, 1979.
9. *Ecclesiae Sanctae*, 34. *Documents on Renewal for Religious*, 86.
10. A list is appended.

Closed	*Sisters reside at:*
1977	
I.H.M., Chester	St. Madeline, Ridley Park
St. Joseph, Mt. Carmel	Our Lady, Mt. Carmel
Our Lady of Pompeii, Phila.	St. Veronica, Phila.
1978	
Seven Dolors, Wyndmoor	I.C., Germantown
Gesu, Phila.	St. Francis Xavier, Phila.
St. Agatha-James, Phila.*	St. Francis de Sales, Phila.
1979	
St. Peter, Elizabethtown	Sacred Heart, Lancaster
St. Nicholas, Weatherly	Little Flower, McAdoo
St. Joseph, Girardville	St. Joseph Ashland
St. Anthony, Phila.	St. Gabriel, Phila.
1980	
St. Ignatius, Centralia	Our Lady, Mt. Carmel

1981
St. Madeline Sophie, Gtn. Immaculate Conception, Gtn.
St. Rose of Lima, Eddystone St. Madeline, Ridley Park

1984
St. Patrick, Norristown Bishop Kenrick, Norristown
St. Margaret Mary, Essington St. Eugene, Primos
Archbishop Prendergast, U.D. Cardinal O'Hara, Springfield

1985
B.V.M., Darby St. Cyril, Lansdowne

*In 1976, St. Agatha and St. James parishes were merged. St. Agatha-James School occupied the facilities of St. James. The sisters resided at St. Agatha until September 1978.

11. *Lumen Gentium*, 6. Abbott, op. cit., 73–4.
12. *Pope John Paul II Speaks to Religious*, 1978–80, 137–8.
13. *Perfectae Caritatis*, 17. *Documents on Renewal for Religious, 86.*
14. *Evangelica Testifictio*, 22. ibid., 225.
15. Pope John Paul II to International Union of Superiors General, Rome, 11/16/78. (Quoted from *Visible Signs of The Gospel*, 28). See also 191, 214, 223.
16. To priests, religious men and women, Maynouth, Ireland, 10/1/79 (quoted in *Visible Signs of The Gospel*, 191).
17. *Documents on Renewal*, (Boston, Daughters of St. Paul, 1974), 281.
18. *Evangelica Testificatio*, 20.
19. V.M.H.S. Archives. Letter to Cardinal Krol from Mother M. Claudia, I.H.M. and Sister Alice Anita, S.S.J.
20. V.M.H.S. Archives. Letter from Cardinal Krol to Mother M. Claudia, August 9, 1971.
21. V.M.H.S Archives. Letter from Bishop Jude Prost, O.F.M., Belém, Pará, Brazil, to Mother M. Claudia, October 2, 1971.
22. *Perfectae Caritatis*, 2. Abbott, op. cit., 468.
23. *Lumen Gentium*, 39.
24. Ibid., 46.
25. *Faithful Witness, Spiritual Conferences*, by Rev. Louis Florent Gillet. (Private Printing, West Chester, Pa., 1947), 181.
26. Ibid., 182.
27. Copy in V.M.H.S. Archives. Original in Monroe Motherhouse Archives.
28. V.M.H.S. Archives. Letter from Cardinal Krol to Mother M. Claudia, February 13, 1976.

29. Rev. Louis Florent Gillet, loc cit, *183–184*.
30. V.M.H.S. Archives. Letter from Most Rev. James Kileen to Mother M. Claudia, August 10, 1976.
31. V.M.H.S. Archives. Letter from Most Rev. Leo Maher to Mother M. Claudia, September 9, 1976.
32. V.M.H.S. Archives. Letter from Bishop R.S. Ndingi Mwana a Nzeki to Mother M. Claudia, September 23, 1976, *cf* Letter, January 27, 1981.
33. V.M.H.S. Archives. Letter from Most Rev. Carlos Oviedo Cavada to Mother M. Claudia, August 20, 1976.
34. V.M.H.S. Archives. Letter from Sister M. Ida to Mother M. Claudia, August 22, 1976.
35. V.M.H.S. Archives. Letter from Monsignor Paul Sheridan, Springfield, Illinois, to Mother M. Claudia, August 22, 1976.
36. V.M.H.S. Archives. Letter from Rev. George Hazler, O.F.M., Pittsburgh, Pennsylvania, to Mother M. Claudia, September 6, 1976.
37. V.M.H.S. Archives. Letter from Monsignor James F. Connelly, Philadelphia, Pennsylvania, to Mother M. Claudia, September 8, 1976.
38. *America*, August 31, 1976, 73.
39. *Perfectae Caritatis*, 15. *Documents on Renewal for Religious*, 85.
40. V.M.H.S. Archives. (Certificates on file).
41. *Perfectae Caritatis*, 13. *Documents on Renewal for Religious*, 82.
42. V.M.H.S. Archives. Letter to Mother Superior from Colonel John F. Denehy, U.S.A.F. Command Chaplain, May 5, 1975.

Chapter 6. Sharing of Witness: Collaboration with Other Religious

1. *Perfectae Caritatis*, 18. *Documents on Renewal for Religious*, 86.
2. *Ecclesiae Sanctae*, 37.
3. *Review for Religious*, Vol. XI (December, 1952), 305.
4. *Review for Religious*, Vol. XI (December, 1952), 225–230.
5. Mother Maria Alma, *Sisters, Servants of the Immaculate Heart of Mary (1845–1967)*, 366.
6. Ibid., 388.
7. *Minutes Region III*, Conference of Major Superiors of Women Religious.
8. V.M.H.S. Archives. Letter from Sister M. Thomas Aquinas Carroll, R.S.M. to Mother M. Claudia, November 16, 1971.
9. Msgr. George A. Kelly, *The Battle for the American Church*, (New York: Doubleday and Co., Inc., 1979), 260–261.

10. Related by Mother M. Claudia in an interview with author, March 16, 1986.
11. Minutes of *Consortium Perfectae Caritatis*.
12. For an appraisal of the *Consortium Perfectae Caritatis*, see Msgr. George Kelly, op. cit., 299–302.
13. V.M.H.S. Archives. Minutes of *Consortium Perfectae Caritatis*.
14. V.M.H.S. Archives. Minutes of Institute on Religious Life.
15. *Consecrated Life*. (Boston, Ma., Daughters of Saint Paul, vol. 9, 2, 1985), Foreword.
16. V.M.H.S. Archives. Letter from Sister Mary Linscott, S.N.D. to Mother M. Claudia, November 22, 1973.
17. V.M.H.S. Archives. Phone call from Secretary of Sacred Congregation of Religious to Mother Marie Genevieve, May 30, 1983.
18. *Ecclesiae Sanctae*, 37. Flannery, op. cit., 632.
19. V.M.H.S. Archives. Letter from Archbishop Henry to Rev. Calthal Coulter, November 15, 1963.
20. V.M.H.S. Archives. Letter from Sister M. Veronica, C.S. to Mother Maria Alma, September 29, 1966.
21. V.M.H.S. Archives. Letter from Archbishop Henry to Rev. Calthal Coulter, November 15, 1963.
22. V.M.H.S. Archives. Letter from Sister Louise, M.S.V., Sister Gerarda, M.S.V., Sister Bianca, M.S.V. to Mother Maria Pacis, October 3, 1963. The congregation originally named the Missionary Sisters of Verona, voted in 1980 to change the title to Comboni Missionary Sisters in honor of their founder.
23. Related by Sister M. Aurora, S.C. to author, March 5, 1985.
24. Sister Virgine, S.C.C. concluded arrangements with Mother M. Claudia on April 10, 1972.
25. They matriculated originally in 1976 after Bishop R.S. Ndigni Nwana Nzeki visited Immaculata during the Eucharistic Congress.
26. Related by Sister Caritas, L.S.O.S.F. to author, March 20, 1986.
27. Related by Sister Dorothy, S.S.J. to author, March 20, 1986.
28. Listed in V.M.H.S. Archives. (Statistics).
29. *Ecclesiae Sanctae*, Flannery, op. cit., 37.
30. "The Image Grows Clear," *Faculty Address* (St. Louis, Queens Work) IV, 11, p. 1.
31. V.M.H.S. Archives. Letter from Archbishop Henry to Rev. Calthal Coulter, November 15, 1963. See also letter from Archbishop Henry to Mother M. Claudia, October 6, 1971.
32. V.M.H.S. Archives. Letter from Archbishop Henry to Mother Maria Pacis, June 3, 1968. See also letter from Archbishop Henry to Mother M. Claudia, March 4, 1970.
33. *Southern Nebraska Register*, August 31, 1984.
34. Brother Raymond Fitz, S.M., and Brother Lawrence Cada, S.M.,

"The Recovery of Religious Life," *Review for Religious*, Vol. 34, 713, September, 1975. See also my response, vol. 35, 287–290, March, 1976.
35. Sister Loretta Gosen, S.PP.S., *Southern Nebraska Register*, September 7, 1984.
36. *Gravissimum Educationis*, 8. Abbott, op. cit., 646.
37. V.M.H.S. Archives. Letter of Mother M. Claudia to Cardinal Krol, August 11, 1976.
38. Sister Loretta Gosen, loc cit.
39. *Entrance to the Kingdom*, 9.
40. V.M.H.S. Archives. Annals, School Sisters of Christ the King.
41. School Sisters of Christ the King Archives, Lincoln, Nebraska.
42. This program was planned in accordance with *Renovationis Causam*, 29.
43. *Southern Nebraska Register*, July 6, 1979.
44. See p. 36 above.
45. V.M.H.S. Archives. School Records.
46. St. Joseph Parish Newsletter, May 6, 1979.
47. V.M.H.S. Archives. Contract, May 20, 1979.
48. V.M.H.S. Archives. Letter of Mother M. Claudia to Sisters, Servants of the Immaculate Heart of Mary, July 1979.
49. In 1981. See p. 31 above.
50. City Council approved a special permit for the construction on December 20, 1983. (See *Lincoln Nebraska Journal*, December 21, 1983).
51. V.M.H.S. Archives. Letter from Rev. James Dawson to Mother Marie Genevieve, December 23, 1983.
52. V.M.H.S. Archives. Annals, St. Joseph, Lincoln, Nebraska.
53. S.S.C.K. Archives.
54. V.M.H.S. Archives Annals, St. Joseph, Lincoln, Nebraska.
55. S.S.C.K. Archives.
56. V.M.H.S. Archives. Letter from Rev. Myron Pleskac to Mother Marie Genevieve, August 18, 1985.
57. *Ecclesiae Sanctae*, 37. *Documents on Renewal for Religious*, 136.

Chapter 7. Facets of Witness: Liturgical Prayer

1. *Sacrosanctum Consilium*, 1. Flannery, op. cit., 1.
2. *Instruction on the Proper Implementation of the Constitution on the Sacred Liturgy*, September 26, 1964, 14, 19. Ibid, 48–9.
3. V.M.H.S. Archives.
4. *Angelus*, September, 1973.
5. V.M.H.S. Archives, Letter from Rev. Lester H. Mitchell, O.F.M. to

Sister Helene Mary, Superior of St. Simon Convent, Los Altos, California, June 30, 1976.
6. Immaculata College Archives.
7. *Sacrosanctum Consilium*, 127.
8. Immaculata College Archives.
9. Immaculata College Bulletin, 1984–1986, 1.
10. See p. 1 above.
11. Pope John Paul II, December 8, 1985. *The Extraordinary Synod*, (Boston, Ma., Daughters of Saint Paul, 1986), 101.

APPENDIX A

Superiors General and Councilors

Date	Superiors General	Sister Assistants and Councilors
1945–1951	M. Maria Alma Ryan	S. Mary Hubert Curran S. Mary Andrew Murray S. Mary Esther Carty S. M. Grace Madeleine Mullarkey
1951–1957	M. Maria Alma Ryan	S. Mary Hubert Curran S. Mary Andrew Murray S. Mary Esther Carty S. M. Paulita Campbell
1957–1962	M. Maria Pacis Dougherty	S. M. Grace Madeleine Mullarkey S. Maria Regina Hoban S. M. Francis Borgia Connors S. M. Franceline Haynes
1962–1968	M. Maria Pacis Dougherty	S. M. Grace Madeleine Mullarkey S. M. Helen Aloysius Hosey S. Mary Hubert Curran S. M. Boniface Carroll
1968–1974	M. M. Claudia Honsberger	S. M. Grace Madeleine Mullarkey S. Margaret Reginia Cunnane

		S. Margaret Mary Baney
		S. Mary Austin Chapman
1974–1981	M. M. Claudia Honsberger	S. Marie Genevieve Lawler
		S. Maria Angelus Finnegan
		S. Margaret Mary Baney
		S. Michael Bernard Dever
1981–	M. Marie Genevieve Lawler	S. Mary Bernard Rapine
		S. Elizabeth Seton Kavanagh
		S. Ann Bernadette MacNamara
		S. Augusta Marie Grant

APPENDIX B

Bachelor Degrees Earned at Immaculata College by Sisters, Servants of the Immaculate Heart of Mary

1925	5		1945	16		1965	54
1926	0		1946	13		1966	108
1927	10		1947	13		1967	134
1928	16		1948	12		1968	210
1929	16——47		1949	13——67		1969	140——646
1930	11		1950	9		1970	157
1931	22		1951	20		1971	141
1932	17		1952	19		1972	104
1933	14		1953	23		1973	80
1934	16——80		1954	34——105		1974	47——529
1935	13		1955	25		1975	22
1936	12		1956	21		1976	7
1937	20		1957	17		1977	35
1938	15		1958	19		1978	15
1939	20——80		1959	22——104		1979	17——96
1940	13		1960	29		1980	10
1941	24		1961	33		1981	20
1942	29		1962	31		1982	13
1943	18		1963	26		1983	14
1944	15——99		1964	39——158		1984	8
						1985	9——74

TOTAL——2,085

APPENDIX C

Master Degrees Earned by Sisters of I.H.M.

		1919	1		
		1920	1		
		1923	1		
		1924	3——6		
1925	2	1945	8	1965	7
1926	1	1946	7	1966	16
1927	0	1947	12	1967	16
1928	1	1948	8	1968	23
1929	1——5	1949	3——38	1969	13——75
1930	3	1950	1	1970	52
1931	4	1951	6	1971	39
1932	2	1952	7	1972	40
1933	10	1953	13	1973	56
1934	10——29	1954	7——34	1974	59——246
1935	2	1955	10	1975	34
1936	2	1956	2	1976	35
1937	8	1957	7	1977	32
1938	3	1958	10	1978	24
1939	4——19	1959	6——35	1979	28——153
1940	3	1960	4	1980	42
1941	12	1961	9	1981	16
1942	13	1962	19	1982	25
1943	16	1963	21	1983	20
1944	8——52	1964	27——80	1984	27
				1985	30——160

TOTAL——932

APPENDIX D

Colleges and Universities Attended by Sisters, Servants of the Immaculate Heart of Mary 1969–85

American
Assumption

Ball State
Barry
Beaver
Bennington
Berkeley
Boston
Bowdoin
Brown
Bryn Mawr
Bucknell
Bucks County

Capitol
Case Western Reserve
Catholic University of American
Catholic University of Chile
Catholic University of Puerto Rico
Central State, Ohio
Clarke

Colby
Columbia
Community, Philadelphia

Dayton
Digby-Stuart
Dillard
Drexel
Duquesne
Dunbarton

East Carolina
East Tennessee
Edinboro

Fordham
Fairleigh-Dickinson

George Mason
George Washington
Georgetown
Georgia State
Glassboro
Gregorian Institute
Gwynedd-Mercy

Holy Cross
Holy Family
Hope
Huston-Tillotson

Indiana
Institut Catholique de Paris

Kansas State
Kutztown

Lake Forest
La Salle
Lehigh
Lincoln
Loyola
Lankenau Hospital
Lynchburg

Marquette
Marymount
Marywood
Miami
Millersville
Montclair State

Newton College of Sacred Heart
North Carolina State
Notre Dame
Notre Dame Pontifical Institute

Oak Ridge
Ohio State
Old Dominion
Oregon College of Education

Peirce Junior
Penn State
Philadelphia Academy of Fine Arts
Philadelphia College of Art
Pratt

Pontifical Catholic University of Peru
Pontifical University of St. Thomas, Rome
Purdue

Regina Mundi, Roma
Rensselaer
Rutgers

San Diego
San Jose
Santa Clara
St. Bonaventure
St. Charles Seminary
College of St. Elizabeth
St. Francis
St. John's University
St. Joseph College, Philadelphia
St. Louis University
St. Michael, Vermont
College of St. Thomas
Scranton University
Seton Hall University
Shippensburg State
Simmons
Stanford
Stonehill

Temple
Tennessee State
Trenton State

University of Bridgeport
University of California
University of Chicago

University of Cincinnati
University of Florida
University of Georgia
University of Illinois
University of Iowa
University of Kentucky
University of Laval
University of Madrid
University of Maine
University of Maryland
University of Mexico
University of Miami
University of Minnesota
University of Missouri
University of New Hampshire
University of North Dakota
University of Oklahoma
University of Pennsylvania
University of Pittsburgh
University of Rhode Island
University of Rochester
University of San Francisco
University of Syracuse
University of Texas
University of Vermont
University of Virginia
University of Washington, D.C.
University of Wisconsin

Vanderbilt
Villanova
Virginia Polytechnical Institute
Virginia State

Washington & Lee
Washington State
Wake Forest
West Chester State
Western Illinois
Western Kentucky
Western Michigan
Westminster, New Wilmington
Wilkes
Winthrop
Wisconsin State

Appendix E

Teacher Certification

February 23, 1981

Ronald Corrigan
Director, Bureau of Teacher Certification
   via: Michael Davis
            Chief Counsel
Nancy K. Matlowski
Counsel for the Department of Education

You have asked for our opinion concerning college credits which may be accepted by the Department for renewal of an Instructional I teaching certificate. Specifically, you have asked for an interpretation of the provisions of 22 Pa. Code 49.84(b) which provides as follows:

> (b) Credits earned in programs designed to prepare for professional fields such as law, medicine, or theology, when relevant to the area of certification, will be considered acceptable for purposes of renewing or converting the Instructional I Certificate.

As I understand the facts, Immaculata College offers courses in theology and religious studies to teachers wishing to use the credits to satisfy the educational requirements for permanent certification. According to Sister Margaret Mary, the courses are undergraduate courses and are offered to members of religious orders as well as lay teachers. Because of the subject matter of the courses the Department has refused to accept the credits for the purpose of permanent certification. It is our opinion that the credits must be accepted by the Bureau of Teacher Certification.

The regulation found at 22 Pa. Code 49.84(b) provides that credits earned in programs designed to prepare for professional fields such a law, medicine, or theology may be accepted only if they are relevant to the area of certification. According to information provided to me, the credits given by Immaculata are not part of any program designed to prepare a person for the professional field of theology or the ministry. The undergraduate credits are given for the purpose of allowing a teacher to secure the credits required for permanent certification.

Because the credits are not part of a program designed to prepare a person for the professional field of theology, the Department lacks the authority to consider the relevancy of the credits to a teacher's area of certification. The regulations provide for a determination of relevancy *only* if the credits are earned in professional programs such as law, medicine, or theology.

In summary, it is our opinion that credits awarded by Immaculata College in theology and religious studies must be accepted by the Department for purposes of permanent certification. I suggest that all certificate holders whose credits were rejected in the past should be notified that their credits will be accepted and applied toward permanent certification.